Boundaries in Recovery
Emotional Sobriety Through Setting Personal Limitations

by Taite Adams

Boundaries in Recovery

Rapid   Response   Press
1730 Lighthouse Terr. S., Suite 12
So   Pasadena,   FL   33707
www.rapidresponsepress.com
Ordering   Information:
Quantity sales. Special discounts are available on quantity purchases by corporations, associations, and others. For details, contact the publisher   at   the   address   above.
Orders by U.S. trade bookstores and wholesalers. Please contact Rapid Response Press: Tel: (866) 983-3025; Fax: (855) 877-4736 or visit www.rapidresponsepress.com.
Printed in the United States of America
Publisher's   Cataloging-in-Publication   data
Adams,   Taite.
A title of a book : a subtitle of the same book / Taite Adams.
p.   cm.
ISBN   978-0-9907674-7-3
1. The main category of the book —Health —Other category. 2. Another subject category —Mind and Body. 3. More categories — Recovery.

First Edition
===================

Limit of Liability/Disclaimer of Warranty

================

Disclaimer

================

Medical Disclaimer

The information contained in this book is not intended to serve as a replacement for professional medical advice. Any use of the information in this book is at the reader's discretion. The author and publisher specifically disclaim any and all liability arising directly or indirectly from the use or application of any information contained in this book. A health care professional should be consulted regarding your specific situation.

To Mom - Thanks for finally saying "No";
To my son - It's a joy to watch you grow up and become your own person;
To my love - Growing and continuing to learn lessons with you beside me is a blessing.

See http://www.TaiteAdams.com for more info

Table of Contents

Preface...1

What are Boundaries?........................3

Types of Boundaries 6

How Boundaries Are Developed........9

Misconceptions About Boundaries 13

Boundaries and Addiction Recovery .15

Unhealthy Boundaries 16

Boundaries and Codependency...19

What are Your Boundaries? 27

The Basics of Setting Limits 33

12 Boundary Guidelines to Live By.....................................39

Emulating Others Healthy Boundaries 44

What Boundaries Are Not 45

Enforcing Your Boundaries...............47

Boundary Violations 48

Honoring and Enforcing Your Boundaries 55

Honoring Others Boundaries...58

Boundaries in Relationships 61

Boundaries in Intimate Relationships 62

Boundaries With Family 72

Boundaries With Children 78

Shifting Boundaries 87
Boundaries and 12 Step Recovery 91
Fellowship as Family 102

Outside Help 104

Living a Healthy Life with Boundaries
....107
Healthy Boundaries 108

Personal Bill of Rights 113

Afterward 117
Resources.....................................119
About the Author.........................123

Preface

The only real conflict you will ever have in your life won't be with others, but with yourself. - Shannon L. Alder

There is little doubt that addiction is an isolating disease, both for the addict and for their loved ones. Even in recovery, a path of destruction has been laid of guilt, shame, fear, sadness and disappointment that takes a great deal of time to repair. While boundaries may have been severely distorted during active addiction, this is often carried over into recovery. As we begin to take responsibility for our choices, one of the areas that bears a significant examination is that of our limitations with others.

Whether in early recovery or sober many years, it often becomes clear that just putting down the drink and the drugs simply isn't enough to live a happy and purposeful life. Those working a solid recovery program have been given some very good tools designed to allow for the examination and change of old ideas, yet boundaries are often an area in recovery that requires ongoing work. Whether due to mixed messages that we received while growing up or simply warped ideas from years of chemical abuse, there's little doubt that our relations with those about us in recovery are our greatest source of ongoing struggle.

One of the cornerstones of long-term recovery is a concept called emotional sobriety. Those of us who wish to remain sober, and happy, should be on a quest of continued growth that includes the ability to regulate emotions. A big part of this is knowing when and how to set appropriate boundaries which, believe it or not, isn't something that many alcoholics inherently know how to do. The good news is that these are skills that can be taught and that is what this book is about,

Boundaries in Recovery

written in the context of boundaries for those in recovery, by someone who has been there and continues to live it on a daily basis.

What are Boundaries?

Boundaries are to protect life, not to limit pleasures. - Edwin Louis Cole

In the simplest terms, boundaries are what set the space between where you end and another person begins. Some like to describe these as lines in the sand but I don't think it's like that at all. Boundaries are much more pliable than an actual demarcation line. They can be re-assessed at will, moved around, and completely erased. Boundaries are definitely limits and before proper limits can be set, one must understand that these have everything to do with how relate to others and the world about us.

Now, anyone who knows even a little bit about an alcoholic or addict probably understands that this isn't necessarily one of their strengths. In fact, many of us spent the end of our drinking and drugging careers in complete isolation, with so many walls thrown up that we thought it might take a lifetime to bring them down. What it really takes is some willingness and a bit of work, but it's so worth it. It soon becomes clear that the causes and conditions underlying much of the destructive behavior are also the key to so much more. I think that the statement from Alcoholics Anonymous' 12&12 Step 4 says it best:

But it is from our twisted relations with family, friends, and society at large that many of us have suffered the most. We have been especially stupid and stubborn about them. The primary fact that we fail to recognize is our total inability to form a true partnership with another human being. Our egomania digs two disastrous pitfalls. Either we insist upon dominating the people we know, or we depend upon them far too much. If we lean too heavily on people, they will sooner or later fail us, for they are human, too, and cannot possibly meet our incessant demands. In this way our insecurity grows and festers. When we habitually try to manipulate others to our own willful desires, they revolt, and resist us heavily. Then we develop hurt feelings, a sense of persecution, and a desire to retaliate. As we redouble our efforts at control, and continue to fail, our suffering becomes acute and constant. We have not once sought to be one in a family, to be a friend among friends, to be a worker among workers, to be a useful member of society. Always we tried to struggle to the top of the heap, or to hide underneath it. This self-centered behavior blocked a partnership relation with any one of those about is. Of true brotherhood we had small comprehension. - 12 Steps & 12 Traditions, P. 53

Whether the controller or the one being controlled (I could be either), instincts gone astray have warped many of our ideas about inter-personal relationships and the need for boundaries. Some of us, myself included, achieve quite a few years of sobriety before it becomes clear that more work needs to be done on emotional sobriety and on boundaries in particular. I love that Bill W. referred to emotional sobriety as "the next frontier" and emphasized relations with others in his famous letter on the subject. As we discuss boundaries, keep this in mind both in the ways in which you can better assert your place in this world and in the various situations that you can begin to be more respectful of others and their limits.

Anne:

In the past few years I was living in almost a passive state of mind. As my using increased I crossed many boundaries. I got so used to this passive state that I forgot what it means to say NO sometimes. I was a "too good friend" as someone said and the best this and that ......meanwhile I forgot where I stand in all this equation. I tolerated many painful situations where drugs were included .I thought that was normal. Now I know it's Not. It's like waking up the morning after a destructive storm. I don't know where should I start fixing my collapsed life. I say collapsed because I find the wreckage of my past catching up with me. I was never like that before. Addiction degrades us into people we barely recognize. I became so arrogant and reckless. I had to do my way at all costs. I forgot what's like to love people (especially my normal friends) without asking them for anything in return or finding them too boring. I find myself still too numb to react to anyone's suffering or pain. I feel as if I'm too exhausted to care anymore.

Types of Boundaries

It is necessary, and even vital, to set standards
for your life and the people you allow in it. –
Mandy Hale

When you have appropriate personal boundaries, you are able to make sound decisions about what types of communication, behavior, and interaction with others are acceptable. The following are the different types of personal boundaries:

Intellectual Boundaries:

Regardless of what you think about recovery or where you live, it's a commonly agreed upon human right that individuals should have the right to think as they please. Taking this a step further, we also have a right to act as we wish as long as it is within the limits of the law. What's key here is that we have to be willing to accept the consequences of these choices. Once understood, there is nothing wrong with wanting to take some time alone with your thoughts in order to get clarity or for having the courage to give your opinion on something that is important to you.

Physical Boundaries:

We all have some semblance of a personal space. Whether you refer to this as your "hula hoop" or something else, physical boundaries refer to what is uniquely "yours" on the material plane. This could relate to both ownership and to the amount of space that we need between our bodies and those of others. Do you know anyone who thinks it's ok to borrow anything you own, no matter the value, whether they ask first or not? These are instances of material boundaries that aren't being well defined or defended.

There can be cultural aspects to the way that this is viewed as North Americans tend to display a greater need for personal space than some other cultures. This is about comfort level and can also encompass a person's views on privacy. Do you ever attend meetings and notice that some people are more comfortable with a handshake or a wave than a hug? This is a physical boundary for them. An aversion to loud music and crowds is another example.

Emotional Boundaries:

Emotional boundaries can be some of the most difficult for those in recovery to identify, establish and defend. That is because so many of us are also incredibly co-dependent. Emotional boundaries distinguish separating your emotions and responsibility for them from someone else's. It's like an imaginary line or force field that separates you and others. Healthy boundaries prevent you from giving advice, blaming or accepting blame. They protect you from feeling guilty for someone else's negative feelings or problems and taking others' comments personally. Good emotional boundaries are non-punitive, and create peaceful connections in which each person feels appreciated and accepted for who he/she is. Don't worry - we are going to discuss how to develop these.

Spiritual Boundaries:

Each person has the right to believe in his/her own spiritual or religious beliefs, especially in recovery. When appropriate spiritual boundaries are in place, there is room for differences in each person's perspective. For many of us, a relationship with a higher power is the basis of our recovery program and it would be a shame to deny someone else of that with our own rigidity. Respect is the basis for the relationship, and there is no hidden (or overt) agenda for changing (or "fixing") the other person's beliefs.

Now that we have an idea of what the different types of boundaries are, let's take a look at how these ideas about limits are developed.

How Boundaries Are Developed

The more severe the dysfunction you experienced growing up, the more difficult boundaries are for you. - David W. Earle

When we discuss what boundaries are, it's helpful to understand how they are formed. Boundaries are, just like most behaviors, learned while we are very young. We learn to "be" in all kinds of relationships by modeling, or by watching how others handle relationships, including those with us. In early childhood, it is our parents, grandparents, siblings, babysitters, teachers, and whoever else we were around on a regular basis that model for us what we believe to be acceptable behavior. As we grow into adolescents, we rely less on parents and more on our friends to help us define ourselves and our boundaries or limits in relationships. However, by that time, a lot of the ingrained behaviors are formed.

I can't count the number of times that I have sat in a meeting and listened to someone share about how their families "just didn't share feelings". This can be a sign of dysfunction or simply a sign of the times. It has been found that how we bond with others is determined by the nature of our bond with our primary care givers. It could be our parents, foster parents or relatives. Anyone raised in the 1970's or earlier was probably raised by a member of the Traditionalist, or Silent, Generation. (I definitely was). This was the generation that grew up through many hardships and that valued privacy above nearly anything else. They worked hard, respected authority, and did not share their inner thoughts and feelings. While respectable values on the surface, the boundaries that are created as a result of this sort of upbringing can be problematic. Obviously, some walls need to crumble and, when they do, most find it very rewarding.

Dysfunction in the home is another story. Unhealthy boundaries could be the result of being raised in a dysfunctional family where maturation and the individuation process was not properly understood. In these types of families, the unmet needs of parents or other adults are sometimes so overwhelming that the task of raising children is demoted to a secondary role. Parents may have been active alcoholics or addicts, could have had underlying psychiatric issues, or some combination thereof. What the children are likely to learn in these situations is that boundaries don't matter, that indeed they, as individual human beings, don't matter except where they are useful for the emotional needs of others. This can lead to a life of enmeshed (meaning no boundaries at all) relationships.

When parents are not able to model healthy boundaries to their children, when their rights are violated, and when they are forced into inappropriate roles with those around them, we tend to have poor boundaries. If children are emotionally neglected, or physically neglected, or abandoned, they may have nonexistent boundaries. If parents fail to nurture them and do not set appropriate limits and discipline, they form weak boundaries too. Due to having a void, they have difficulty forming a sense of "self."

As they grow up in their families of origin in these sorts of situations, they lack the support they need from parents or caregivers to form a healthy sense of their own identities. their own individuality. In fact, they may learn that to get their needs met they must get their way with others. To do this they need to intrude on the emotional boundaries of other people just as their father or mother may have done. They would in all likelihood grow up with fluid boundaries, that cause them to swing between feelings of engulfment on the one hand and abandonment on the other, inevitably leading to dysfunctional relationships later on in life. They would have at best, a hazy sense of their own personal boundaries, not able to properly define where they end and the other begins.

Conversely, they may learn that rigid and inflexible boundaries might be the way to handle their relationships with other people. They wall themselves off in their relationships as a way of protecting their emotional selves and, as a consequence, will in all likelihood find it difficult to form lasting close interpersonal bonds with others in adulthood as they are still trying to individuate from their parents. (Remember that quote from Chapter 1?) The exception in this is of relationships predicated on the same rigid rule based structure as their family of origin where nothing came into the family or out from it, but in this case the bond is likely to be enmeshment.

Research shows that abuse, humiliation, or shame cause a great deal of damage to boundaries (this is discussed again later on). Also, inappropriate generational roles among family members, and inappropriate roles between our family and other families, can also damage boundary formation. People, who have been in the role of care takers, begin to believe other people's thoughts, feelings, and problems are their responsibility. Care taking also damages boundaries.

Controlling people also tend to trespass other people's boundaries and the person who is being controlled, will fail to have rights to his or her emotions, thoughts, and privacy.

While some of these descriptions sound a bit bleak, it has been my experience that once we understand where we're at and how we got there, we have a much better chance of finding the door. For anyone who feels that they are stuck with some really unhealthy boundaries, for whatever reason, don't despair. You are definitely not alone.

Elizabeth:

As a child I was a victim but as an adult I was more like a volunteer because I choose to stay in sick relationships, friendships and/or otherwise. I quickly had to let go of the idea that 'people walked all over me' because I was the one lying down! So boundaries for me are about taking care of myself and keeping the focus on myself, they are not a tool I use to manipulate others to my will or as a way of controlling another. I.e. If I am in a situation and feel I am being abused, I leave the situation. What the other person chooses to do about me leaving is none of my business. They may say sorry and ask me to return and amend their behavior or they may not. I.e. I don't speak on the phone after a certain time at night, so rather than answer the phone and have to tell people this, again and again then get upset with them, I don't answer the phone. Boundaries make my life less complicated and encourage me to practice new behavior.

Misconceptions About Boundaries

Setting boundaries is a way of caring for myself. It doesn't make me mean, selfish, or uncaring because I don't do things your way. I care about me too. – Christine Morgan

There is a popular line of books on the market about Boundaries that seems to do quite well but that is a bit too Biblical for my taste. One of the things that *Cloud and Townsend* have provided that I love, however, is their list of myths about boundaries. I don't know about you but I came into recovery with all sorts of false ideas that had to be discarded. Many of them had to do with my place in this world and how I relate to others. Here are some common misconceptions about boundaries:

- **If I Set Boundaries, I'm Being Selfish** (selfishness actually has to do with the fixation on our own wishes and desires to the exclusion of our responsibility to love others)

- **If I Began Setting Boundaries, I Will Be Hurt by Others** (Those people in our lives who can respect our boundaries will love our wheels, our opinions, our separateness)

- **If I Set Boundaries, I Will Hurt Others** (Appropriate boundaries don't control, attack or hurt anyone. They simply prevent you from being taken advantage of)

- **Boundaries Mean That I Am Angry** (Boundaries don't cause anger in us. Anger can tell us that our boundaries have

~ 13 ~

been violated and it can tell us if we're in danger of being controlled)

- **When Others Set Boundaries, It Injures Me** (An inability to accept other's boundaries can indicate a problem in taking responsibility. Some people become so accustomed to others rescuing them that they begin to believe that their well-being is someone else's problem. They feel let down and unloved when they aren't bailed out. They fail to accept responsibility for their own lives. Do you want others to respect your boundaries? Then you must be willing to respect the boundaries of others.)

- **Boundaries Cause Feelings of Guilt** (One of the major obstacles to setting boundaries is our feeling of obligation. Many people solve this dilemma by avoiding setting boundaries with those to whom they may feel an obligation)

- **Boundaries Are Permanent, and I'm Afraid of Burning My Bridges** (It's important to understand that if you set limits with someone and he/she responds maturely and lovingly, you can renegotiate the boundary if appropriate)

- **Love has no boundaries** (Sometimes the most loving gesture is to say no. For instance, when your husband has just gotten his 3rd DUI and calls to ask you to come and bail him out. Many of us know from experience that this sort of enabling doesn't work, no matter how much we might love someone.)

Boundaries and Addiction Recovery

The boundary to what we can accept is the boundary to our freedom. – Tara Brach

I know that when I was in active addiction, boundaries were not something that I ever thought of. In the years when I was still social and able to participate in the party scene, boundaries were either blurred or non-existent. I became entirely too close with people I didn't even know and put myself in some very precarious circumstances. In later years, it was quite the opposite. I had been hurt by enough people and suffered enough consequences from my addiction that I found it was better to just shut the doors, both literally and figuratively, and go it alone.

When I got sober, continuing to live at either of these extremes wasn't going to be very productive, yet many of the behaviors continued. I had a habit of forming relationships too quickly, saying "yes" to anyone and everyone, and then pushing people away when I got scared. Understandably, I had no sense of identity and was pretty terrified that continuing to practice my past behaviors would lead me back to drugs and alcohol. There are several ways to improve boundaries, but what worked for me was that inherent feeling that a lot of the things that I was continuing to do were not serving my greatest good. Granted, not everyone gets these intuitive nudges and many of mine came over the course of several years, so let's discuss what exactly unhealthy boundaries really are.

Unhealthy Boundaries

*Whatever you are willing to put up with, is
exactly what you will have.*

When I think of unhealthy boundaries, I go back to that lengthy quote in the first chapter that tells us how we are "unable to form a true partnership with another human being". While there are exceptions to this and some long-standing relationships with people that come into recovery, there is no doubt that, as a whole, we are not our true selves and most of us have no idea what that concept even means in the beginning. Not sure if your boundaries are healthy or not? Here is a pretty substantial list of unhealthy boundaries:

- I let others direct my life.

- I let others define me.

- I feel as if my happiness depends on other people.

- It's hard for me to look a person in the eye.

- I have difficulty saying "no" to people.

- I find myself getting involved with people who end up hurting me.

- I trust others without reason.

- I would rather attend to others than attend to myself.

- I think other's opinions are more important than mine.

- People take or use my things without asking me.

- I have difficulty asking for what I want or need.

- I lend people money and don't seem to get it back.

- I'd rather go along with others than to express what I'd prefer to do.
- I tend to stay in relationships that are hurting me.
- I feel empty, as if something is missing in my life.
- I tend to get caught "in the middle" of other people's problems.
- When someone I'm with acts up in public, I tend to feel embarrassed.
- I prefer to rely on what others say about what I should believe or do.
- I tend to take on or feel what others are feeling.
- I seem to put more into relationships than I get out of them.
- I feel responsible for other people's feelings.
- I easily tell all.
- I talk at an intimate level in a first meeting.
- I easily fall in love with a new acquaintance.
- I easily fall in love with someone who reaches out to me.
- I am easily overwhelmed by a person/ easily preoccupied.
- I go against personal values or rights to please others.
- I accept food, gifts, touch, or sex that I don't want.
- I don't notice when someone else displays inappropriate boundaries.
- I don't notice when someone invades my boundaries.
- I touch people without asking.

Boundaries in Recovery

- I allow others to touch me without asking.

- I take as much as I can get for the sake of getting.

- I give as much as I can give for the sake of giving.

- I allow others to take as much as they want from me.

- I believe others can or should anticipate my needs.

- I expect others to fill my needs automatically.

- I fall apart so someone will take care of me.

- I abuse food or other substances.

- I continue to put myself in drinking and drugging situations.

- I can't make up my mind.

Don't be discouraged if you answered in the affirmative to many of these. Even someone with many years of sobriety who is working a good program probably displays a few of these traits from time to time. I certainly do. A common thread throughout these reveals that having unhealthy boundaries is closely correlated codependency and self-esteem.

Boundaries and Codependency

Givers need to set limits because takers rarely do. - Rachel Wolchin

The term *codependency* has been around for almost four decades. Although it originally applied to spouses of alcoholics, first called co-alcoholics, researchers revealed that the characteristics of codependents were much more prevalent in the general population than had been imagined. In fact, they found that if you were raised in a dysfunctional family or had an ill parent, you're likely codependent. It's become pretty evident to me over the years that many, many people in recovery also have codependency issues. The following is a list of symptoms of codependents. You don't have to exhibit all of these symptoms to qualify.

- **Low self-esteem**. Feeling that you're not good enough or comparing yourself to others are signs of low self-esteem. The tricky thing about self-esteem is that some people think highly of themselves, but it's only a disguise — they actually feel unlovable or inadequate. Ever heard the saying, "An alcoholic is an egomaniac with an inferiority complex." ? Underneath, usually hidden from consciousness, are feelings of shame. Guilt and perfectionism often go along with low self-esteem. If everything is perfect, you don't feel bad about yourself.

- **People-pleasing**. It's fine to want to please someone you care about, but codependents usually don't think they have a choice. Saying "No" causes them anxiety. Some codependents have a hard time saying "No" to anyone. They go out of their way and sacrifice their own needs to accommodate other people.

- **Poor boundaries**. This is an area where codependents especially get into trouble. They have blurry or weak boundaries. They feel responsible for other people's feelings and problems or blame their own on someone else. Some codependents have rigid boundaries. They are closed off and withdrawn, making it hard for other people to get close to them. Sometimes, people flip back and forth between having weak boundaries and having rigid ones.

- **Reactivity**. A consequence of poor boundaries is that you react to everyone's thoughts and feelings. If someone says something you disagree with, you either believe it or become defensive. You absorb their words, because there's no boundary. With a boundary, you'd realize it was just their opinion and not a reflection of you and not feel threatened by disagreements.

- **Caretaking**. Another effect of poor boundaries is that if someone else has a problem, you want to help them to the point that you give up yourself. It's natural to feel empathy and sympathy for someone, but codependents start putting other people ahead of themselves. In fact, they need to help and might feel rejected if another person doesn't want help. Moreover, they keep trying to help and fix the other person, even when that person clearly isn't taking their advice.

- **Control**. Control helps codependents feel safe and secure. Everyone needs some control over events in their life. You wouldn't want to live in constant uncertainty and chaos, but for codependents, control limits their ability to take risks and share their feelings. Sometimes they have an addiction that either helps them loosen up, like alcoholism, or helps them hold their feelings down, like workaholism, so that they don't feel out of control. Codependents also need to control those close to them, because they need other people to behave in a certain way to feel okay. In fact, people-pleasing and care-taking can be used to control and manipulate people. Alternatively, codependents can be bossy and tell you what you should or shouldn't do. This is a violation of someone else's boundary.

- **Dysfunctional communication**. Codependents have trouble when it comes to communicating their thoughts, feelings and needs. Of course, if you don't know what you think, feel or need, this becomes a problem. Other times, you know, but you won't own up to your truth. You're afraid to be truthful, because you don't want to upset someone else. Instead of saying, "I don't like that," you might pretend that it's okay or tell someone what to do. Communication becomes dishonest and confusing when you try to manipulate the other person out of fear.

- **Obsessions**. Codependents have a tendency to spend their time thinking about other people or relationships. This is caused by their dependency and anxieties and fears. They can also become obsessed when they think they've made or might make a "mistake."Sometimes you can lapse into fantasy about how you'd like things to be or about someone you love as a way to avoid the pain of the present. This is one way to stay in denial, discussed below, but it keeps you from living your life.

- **Dependency**. Codependents need other people to like them to feel okay about themselves. They're afraid of being rejected or abandoned, even if they can function on their own. Others need to always be in a relationship, because they feel depressed or lonely when they're by themselves for too long. This trait makes it hard for them to end a relationship, even when the relationship is painful or abusive. They end up feeling trapped.

- **Denial.** One of the problems people face in getting help for codependency is that they're in denial about it, meaning that they don't face their problem. Usually they think the problem is someone else or the situation. They either keep complaining or trying to fix the other person, or go from one relationship or job to another and never own up the fact that they have a problem. Codependents also deny their feelings and needs. Often, they don't know what they're feeling and are instead focused on what others are feeling. The same thing goes for their needs. They pay attention to other people's needs and not their own. They might be in denial of their need for space and autonomy. Although some codependents seem needy, others act like they're self-sufficient when it comes to needing help. They won't reach out and have trouble receiving. They are in denial of their vulnerability and need for love and intimacy.

- **Problems with intimacy.** By this I'm not referring to sex, although sexual dysfunction often is a reflection of an intimacy problem. I'm talking about being open and close with someone in an intimate relationship. Because of the shame and weak boundaries, you might fear that you'll be judged, rejected, or left. On the other hand, you may fear being smothered in a relationship and losing your autonomy. You might deny your need for closeness and feel that your partner wants too much of your time; your partner complains that you're unavailable, but he or she is denying his or her need for separateness.

- **Painful emotions.** Codependency creates stress and leads to painful emotions. Shame and low self-esteem create anxiety and fear about being judged, rejected or abandoned; making mistakes; being a failure; feeling trapped by being close or being alone. The other symptoms lead to feelings of anger and resentment, depression, hopelessness, and despair. When the feelings are too much, you can feel numb.

Codependency is an addiction, an addiction to dangerously self-gratifying behaviors that inevitably trap the codependent individual in unhealthy situations. Codependents are people who are addicted to "helping" others without regard for their own desires and needs. If these symptoms don't grab you (they do me), we as codependents also have a tendency to take on a variety of roles to fulfill our needs. These include:

- **The Martyr** - To suffer is virtuous, especially when you put others' needs ahead of your own. At least that's the message you may have received from your family, religious institution, or cultural heritage. At work, you're always the first to pick up an extra project and the last to leave the office, deciding to skip the gym when a friend wants company. You pick up the tab, unasked, even when you're broke. You take on any and all service positions, even when not asked. When sacrifice is a way of being, you neglect your own needs to receive love and care. Yet, paradoxically, that's precisely what you are trying to get by jockeying for others' appreciation or indebtedness. The approach usually backfires: Not only do you begin to resent those you've helped (who never seem to return the favor), but your so-called beneficiaries either take your suffering for granted (you've trained them well!) or begin to resent you right back.

- **The Savior** - The world is a dangerous place! Fortunately, you are here to save the day. When your friend is short of rent money (again), you float her a little cash (again) so she can make ends meet. You perform 12-Step calls on the homeless daily, even though they have made it clear that they don't want what you have. What is the problem here? Yes, it's true that everyone needs help sometimes. But when you feel personally responsible for another person's comfort and well-being, you strip her of the opportunity to create her own comfort and well-being. You enable self-limiting behavior and effectively tell someone she is helpless without you. In time, she may even come to believe this.

- **The Adviser** - If you were a character in a Peanuts comic strip, it would be Lucy, sitting behind her makeshift desk offering advice about anything for a nickel. Indeed, you may have an uncanny ability to see straight into another person's problems and offer clear counsel. Or you may just think you have great insight and regularly volunteer your sponsorship services to anyone who walks by. Listening might not be your greatest strength. This is a case where it truly takes two to tango: We may think of the person who constantly seeks advice as the one who lacks self-esteem. But people who feel compelled to perpetually advise and control others are equally insecure. If you are peddling your sponsorship wares with abandon, consider that there may be an issue here.

- **The People Pleaser** - You enjoy volunteering at your home group's picnic and monthly anniversary dinner. You don't mind making the Friday coffee run for your colleagues. It's especially nice when you feel the love, basking in the attention and praise that come with your generosity. But being nice can have a dark side. You know you've found that dark side when you feel that your gifts aren't adequately appreciated, or when the thought of volunteering at another event seems more chore than joy. You really know you've found it when you use your people-pleasing skills to control others, believing they will like you for the favors you do rather than for who you are. "People pleasing is a very passive form of manipulation," says Marc Hertz, a St. Paul, Minn.–based consultant in the addiction and recovery field. "We often do things for others to get what we want or need from them."

- **The Yes-Person** - You say yes to a friend when you mean no, then resent it. You smile in faux agreement with your friend rather than say what you feel. You maintain détente with your partner, but you never admit when you're upset. Feelings of resentment build up until you feel as if you're going to explode. "[Couples] tell me 'We never fight' and look at me like they want my approval," says Julie Sullivan, LCMFT, founder of Looking Glass Therapy and Mediation Center in Leawood, Kan.. In her opinion, a total absence of conflict means an erosion of honesty.

If you see yourself in any of these roles, a hearty congrats. Awareness is a critical first step to growth and change. I'm sure it's not the first time you've heard that tidbit. With regards to boundaries, things can get complicated (and painful) because this is another instance of letting go of old ideas. One of the first steps towards lasting change is to take a look at what your specific boundaries and values really are.

What are Your Boundaries?

Confront the dark parts of yourself, and work to banish them with illumination and forgiveness. Your willingness to wrestle with your demons will cause your angels to sing. - August Wilson

Those of us working a solid recovery program are no strangers to inventories and that is exactly what this is. In order for you to move forward and begin to set some limits, you need to find out where you're at. This means taking an honest look at your own boundaries, or lack thereof, and how you relate to boundaries in general. This will give you an idea of how healthy and empowering your boundaries really are, whether they are serving or endangering your recovery program, and even your attitudes towards boundaries themselves.

The thing about boundaries is that most of us could use improvement in nearly all areas. They are often either too rigid or not strong enough. Sometimes we hear about people who put up walls. I know that I have been described as one of these people. This means that a person doesn't show much outward emotion towards others and may set some strong physical boundaries. Maybe they don't hug, touch, or even participate in social activities as much as others, coming off as "hard".

Those who put up walls may think that they are protecting themselves from repeating hurts of the past, but this is flawed logic. When walls are kept up like this, it becomes difficult for a person to simply relax and enjoy life as they are in a constant state of worry and mistrust. Unhappiness actually results from the walls and isn't prevented by them. This is why it's important to take a look at areas in your life where you may be putting up too many walls, or setting too rigid of boundaries. Let's start there.

If you own a journal, this would be a good time to get it out for a bit of writing. Thinking about these sorts of things is great but nothing produces greater results than by putting them down in black and white. Here are the things that you should take some notes on:

EXAMPLE:

In what areas am I setting too many boundaries?

1)___friendships_____

Reason: ___broken confidences in the past_____

Effects: ___self-esteem, personal relationships, pride_____

In what areas am I setting too many boundaries?

1)_____

Reason: _____

Effects: _____

In what areas am I setting too many boundaries?

2)_____

Reason: _____

Effects: _____

In what areas am I setting too many boundaries?

3)_____

Reason: _____

Effects: _____

In what areas am I setting too many boundaries?

4)_____

Reason: _____

Effects: _____

...keep going until you are finished.

At the opposite end of the spectrum is a lack of boundaries in various areas of life that is sure to lead to a great deal of anxiety and stress. Whether developed, or not developed, due to childhood trauma or related issues with addiction, there is no doubt that the constant "over-giving", "over-committing", and "over-accommodating" is not conducive to true emotional sobriety, yet it's tough behavior to change. As many who lack boundaries tend to be attracted to people who will dominate them, the scenario is one that will continue to bring stress and pain. The first step is to take a look at the areas in your life that need to be addressed.

EXAMPLE:

In what areas am I not setting boundaries?

1)_____sexual_____

Reason: __I still seek attention even though it isn't genuine__

Effects: __self-esteem, personal relationships, sex relations__

In what areas am I not setting boundaries?

1)_____

Boundaries in Recovery

Reason: _____

Effects: _____

In what areas am I not setting boundaries?

2)_____

Reason: _____

Effects: _____

In what areas am I not setting boundaries?

3)_____

Reason: _____

Effects: _____

In what areas am I not setting boundaries?

4)_____

Reason: _____

Effects: _____

...keep going until you are finished.

This should give you a great start as a base-line for what areas you need to take a look at and the underlying cause of some of your boundary issues. If you are not sure you are good at setting boundaries or indeed have any at all, ask yourself these questions.

- How often do I worry about what other people think?

- Do I feel guilty for wanting to do things by myself?

- When did I last say no to someone?

- When did I last say yes to something I secretly didn't want to do?

- Do I feel like I deserve respect or I have to earn it by being 'nice'?

- What are the five rules to being my friend? Do I know them quickly and easily?

- What are the 10 things I most like to do with my time? Can I quickly come up with them?

- What are the 10 things I hate doing? Do I even have strong feelings about things?

- When I think about saying no to someone, do I feel afraid? Or calm inside?

As an additional exercise in your boundary inventory, try the following:

Start noticing (and keeping a list of) the people and activities that energize you, and those that drain you. This is a great exercise that offers some clear perspective when done over a period of time. Whenever I've had an interaction that drains me I make a note of it in my journal, as I do for experiences that energize me. I've found it really helpful in identifying what I need to do to protect my energy and then focusing on operating in environments and situations that strengthen me instead of drain me.

Make a list of specific relationships that have become stressful or draining for you, and see if you can identify when it was that you

allowed a boundary to be crossed. For example, you might be starving for an evening off yet you committed every Thursday until Christmas to something you don't really want to do, because you were scared to offend the person who begged you to volunteer for their cause. If something is draining you or making you resentful, it's not necessarily the person or situation's fault - it could likely be your fault, for not putting boundaries around the person or situation that honor your own true needs.

When you feel compelled to binge on unhealthy foods, or drink alcohol, or go shopping (or anything else you use to numb your feelings) try to identify what brought it on. (These are sometimes called "triggers"). If your urge followed an interaction with someone, or a certain situation in your life, try to identify what specifically upsets you about it and what you could do to change it in the future. When you're tempted to numb out with food or some other compulsive behavior, use it to learn more about what is causing you distress and how you could change that.

Get clear about what a protected, on-purpose life would look and feel like. In your journal, describe what a "just-right" life would be composed of. Who would you be spending time with? What activities would you be involved with? In what way would you find time to express what you believe to be your purpose in life? How much alone time, fun time, play time would you have? Once you've written this out, identify the people and activities in your life that are making it hard or even impossible to live the way you deeply long to. See what you can do to clear out time you need, right now.

You can change your life into something that feels right for you. You are here for a reason, and we need you to be at your best. We need you to be rested, and to have time available to do what you were put on this earth to do, no matter how big or small. You need time for you and for those you love most, in order for you to be happy and healthy and a blessing to all of us. This is really important, it isn't selfish.

The Basics of Setting Limits

'No' is a complete sentence. — Anne Lamott

The purpose of having boundaries is to protect and take care of ourselves. A first step is knowing that we actually have a right to protect and defend ourselves. Taking it a step further, we not only have the right, but a duty to take responsibility for how we allow others to treat us. If you are in recovery, some semblance of self-esteem has likely been established, or re-established, through the act of getting clean and sober. Most of us still had some work to do with regards to our relationships with others, however, and boundaries are a big part of that.

A large part of setting boundaries deals with identifying and getting rid of old ideas about what is acceptable in human relationships. This often requires us to not only take another look at our past, but to also be able to identify feelings and emotions so that they can be expressed properly when we communicate with others. For anyone accustomed to being accommodating, compliant, or shut off from the world, the process of setting and implementing boundaries may feel threatening and unnatural at first. That's ok because it's new! As you begin to stand up for yourself and your limits, you will feel increasingly empowered and confident. You will like and respect yourself more and others will be attracted to your authenticity and self-confidence.

Here's how to set boundaries:

Mind Shift - Begin with the mind shift that having personal boundaries is ok. It doesn't mean that you are selfish or unloving. It is both completely acceptable and absolutely necessary for healthy relationships. Understand that self-worth comes from defining your life as you want it to be, not from the acceptance or identity of others.

Define - Sit down and think about how you have been allowing others to take advantage of you and how you might be accepting situations that are really unacceptable to you. Make a list of things that people may no longer do to you, say to you, or do around you. Decide how you need physical and emotional space. Define your values, belief system, and outlook on life so you have a clear picture of who you are and how you want to live. This is an extension of what we did in the last chapter (Boundaries Inventory). Get very clear on this.

Communicate - Sit down with the people involved in crossing your personal boundaries and kindly communicate your mind shift. Let them know you have spent some time thinking about what is important and acceptable to you and what isn't. Let them know how they have crossed your boundaries in the past, and ask them to respect and support your new boundaries.

This is probably one of the most difficult parts of setting boundaries for most people. It's all well and good to decide how you want to be treated, but to communicate this to someone else in a healthy manner is something else entirely. It is important to communicate boundaries clearly, concisely, and without apology. When appropriate, use "I statements" to keep the focus on yourself and keep the other person from becoming defensive. "I feel frustrated/angry when you _____ or when xyz happens". I don't know about you but I am always struggling to come up with proper "feeling" words to label my various emotions. Below is a great list to help with that.

Once you are able to communicate a boundary, it is oftentimes necessary to set consequences as well. Never state something that you are not willing to follow through with. To set boundaries and not enforce them just gives the other person an excuse to continue with the same old behavior. For example: "I feel anxious when you yell like that. I'd prefer to talk about things in a calm manner. If it happens again, I'll have to leave the room." Not all boundaries need to be stated in this form, however. Simple, direct, statements also work just fine. Here are a few examples.

- "It's hard for me to concentrate when I'm on the phone, could you wait til I'm done before asking me questions?"
- "I'm not willing to argue with you."

- "I love you and I'm not willing to get into a car with you when you've been drinking."
- "I want to hear about your day. I'll be free to give you my full attention in 15 minutes."
- "I'm sorry; that doesn't work for me. I won't be loaning you money until you have paid me what I loaned you previously."

Here are some other great examples of boundaries using simple, direct language:

- *To set a boundary with an angry person:*
  "You may not yell at me. If you continue, I'll have to leave the room."

- *To set a boundary with personal phone calls at work:*
  "I've decided to take all personal calls in the evening in order to get my work done. I will need to call you later."

- *To say no to extra commitments:*
  "Although this organization is important to me, I need to decline your request for volunteer help in order to honor my family's needs."

- *To set a boundary with someone who is critical:*
  "It's not okay with me that you comment on my weight. I'd like to ask you to stop."

- *To buy yourself time when making tough decisions:*
  "I'll have to sleep on it, I have a policy of not making decisions right away."

- *To back out of a commitment:*
  "I know I agreed to head up our fundraising efforts, but after

reviewing my schedule, I now realize that I won't be able to give it my best attention. I'd like to help find a replacement by the end of next week.

- *To set a boundary with an adult child who has a drug problem:*
  "I won't be enabling you anymore. I love you and you need to take responsibility for yourself."

Expect - Expect that these conversations will feel uncomfortable and difficult, especially if you are a pleaser. There may be some defensiveness and push-back from those involved. That's OK. They'll get used to your new boundaries over time. Be aware that some people in your life may fall away as a result of your new outlook and demand for respect. But these aren't people you want in your life anyway. You will find you attract new, supportive, and healthy-minded people into your life as you continue to grow. Whatever you do, don't compromise your values, integrity, and self-respect simply to keep someone in your life. Your soul can't sustain that.

When you begin to set boundaries, do not justify, get angry, or apologize for the boundary you are setting. You are not responsible for the other person's reaction to the limits you are establishing. You are only responsible for communicating your boundary in a respectful manner. If it upset them, know it is their problem. Some people, especially those accustomed to controlling, abusing, or manipulating you, might test you. Plan on it, expect it, but remain firm. Remember, your behavior must match the boundaries you are setting. You cannot successfully establish a clear boundary if you send mixed messages by apologizing.

YOU'RE EVOLVED AND GROUNDED
AND IN CONTROL OF YOUR LIFE AND I
JUST FIND THAT VERY INCONSIDERATE.

12 Boundary Guidelines to Live By

Daring to set boundaries is about having the courage to love ourselves, even when we risk disappointing others. - Brene Brown

Many people just want some clear gut guidelines to get them started with boundaries. If the previous ideas about the process of setting limits weren't enough to get you started, here are twelve pretty solid guidelines when it comes to boundaries:

1. Don't give access to yourself when you first meet someone, but do so only very gradually. While you can be friendly and polite, be more thoughtful about opening up completely. Open up 20% instead of 80% until you have a good sense of the person. If you don't open up too quickly, there's no need to shut down the energy as dramatically if things get uncomfortable. People are more likely to be offended if you are very warm and open, and then cool off suddenly. Take your time.

2. Recognize and respect your own needs, desires, and comfort zone. Some people are so concerned with pleasing others, they don't check in with their inner compass to find out what their own needs are - a need for respect, quiet, personal power, support, kindness, solitude, free choice, etc. The earlier you are aware of your own comfort zone, the less likely you will let people go too far.

3. Tune down your energy. When you feel discomfort around someone intrusive, whether they are rude or overly friendly, cool down your energy. Be less open and receptive. You can subtly withdraw energy from the other person through posture, tone of voice, facial expression - particularly the eyes. For instance, look at the person less or with less personal warmth.

4. Cool gently or suddenly: If someone is generally well-intentioned and you don't want to hurt his or her feelings, withdraw energy gently. That person will often sense it without consciously knowing what's going on. If someone doesn't sense your subtle withdrawal, withdraw more energy. If you still feel uncomfortable, you can verbalize your boundaries. For example, at a social gathering, "I'm sorry, I came here to spend time with a friend tonight." Then turn away, or you can always leave.

5. Refrain from being 100% open about every feeling and thought even with close friends, children and partners. Keep parts of yourself to yourself. This can be difficult for some in early recovery because we mistake being "honest" with being an open book with everyone we meet. You can be kind without being completely open (and therefore vulnerable). Take care of your precious vulnerability/inner child/inner life spark as if it were life itself, because it is. You don't want to lock away that part of yourself, but be SELECTIVE in when, with whom and how much you share of it. Make it a conscious choice from moment to moment. You are never obligated to answer anybody's questions. When confronted, feel free to counter with another question, "Why do you ask?" Or, "I'd rather talk about something else right now."

6. Express what you want in a positive way. With friends and family, it's important to express your feelings. If you feel a need for boundaries, state your specific needs and make specific positive requests. Examples:

- "I need to be alone right now."
- "I need to calm down."
- "I'm willing to talk to you if you would be polite."
- "I'd like to figure this out myself. You may be right, but life is more enjoyable when we make our own mistakes."
- "I'd like it if you didn't speak to me with that tone of voice."

- To your child: "I really enjoy spending time with you. I also need a little time alone to re-energize. So I'll spend an hour reading and then you can help me in the kitchen."

7. Be less reactive. Keep some feelings and ideas to yourself, OR, if you express them, do so from a place of calm. This is the opposite of being drawn into argument and being reactive. Having boundaries means not being reactive or fused (enmeshed) to the other person. It means not needing the other person's understanding and permission, but knowing what you want and calmly going after it. Often, the more you demand and insist on boundaries in an angry or pleading manner, the clearer it is that you are not in control of yourself or your boundaries.

Imagine an intrusive friend says angrily, "Why don't you just do it the way I told you!" An over-reactive response would be to say angrily, "Stop telling me what to do! You have no idea what I'm going through." The better response would be to say calmly, "I appreciate your desire to help. But it would be more helpful right now if you didn't make suggestions."

8. Limit intrusive and draining phone calls and conversations, particularly venting, gossip, and complaints. Some healthy responses might be:

- "Unfortunately, I have to get going. Talk to you soon." "Hi. I only have a minute." One minute later, "I have to go. Good luck/ Have a great afternoon."
- If it's an ongoing problem that you'd like to address: "I feel a bit drained when we talk about these problems so much. I'd prefer to talk about something more uplifting."
- "Although I like to connect with you, I don't have time to for long phone conversations, given my work and kids."
- "I'm sorry you're going through so much. I'd like to know what you want from me. Do you want advice? Do you want me to

point out how you might be participating in this ongoing pattern?" If the answer is NO, you can say, "Then I'm afraid I can't be of any help to you."

9. Don't take without asking. Taking food off someone's plate without asking is an example of fused behavior to avoid. People often feel it's intimate and romantic to take food off each other's plate. The "what's mine is yours" mentality does lead to closeness, but not the type that's desirable. Emotional and physical fusion lead to control issues and resentment. Only when people remain emotionally and physically separate can they truly become more intimate. If you wish to achieve the best form of intimacy (whether between lovers, friends, parent and child) be sure to first ask, "May I try a bite?"

10. Respect another person's body as well as your own. No matter how many years you've been married, you are separate individuals, physically and emotionally. Acting as though the other person belongs to you leads to lack of respect, lack of passion, and degradation. Strive to be an honored guest, not an uninvited one. Always seek permission when you touch someone. This doesn't necessarily mean asking permission with words, but look for the energy and body language that says, "yes."

11. Respect a child's autonomy regarding his or her body. This teaches the child ownership of his or her body. A child who is brought up with parents who dress the child beyond an appropriate age, impose unwanted affection, or don't respect the child's privacy, for example, does not learn to sense when his or her boundaries are being encroached.

12. Be respectful and expect respect both in public and at home. People who are critical or bicker in public are self-demeaning and irritating to be with. If a child, friend, or partner is inappropriately rude in private or public, it's important to express yourself calmly and firmly and be willing to leave if necessary. Public humiliation requires

immediate attention. If someone criticizes or mocks you in public (or in private), you might say calmly but seriously, "When you say that, I feel uncomfortable/sad/angry and want to leave. Please don't do that." If the person continues, it's important to be willing to calmly leave the situation - the restaurant or eventually the relationship. Once boundaries are established, they are less likely to be encroached upon.

Emulating Others Healthy Boundaries

When trying to teach someone a boundary,
they learn less from the enforcement of the
boundary and more from the way the
boundary was established. – Bryant H. McGill

When we are learning new, healthy, behaviors it always helps to have a good example in front of us. I know that in getting sober, that example was a sponsor and a group of responsible, sober, women who I chose to start spending time with, observing and emulating. Being around people who were living the way that I aspired to live my life made making some difficult changes a bit easier. They were not only good examples for me, but also great cheerleaders and advocates in times of struggle. These sorts of role models can work with emotional sobriety and boundaries as well.

Is there someone in your life that you feel has really healthy boundaries? Maybe there are several people that you respect and admire who have really figured out how to set limits in some key areas in their lives and are reaping the rewards. These are the people that you will want to observe and emulate as you embark on your journey to establish and defend your new healthy boundaries. It may help if you approach these people and let them know what it is that you are doing, lest you end up violating their well-established boundaries. Whether you do or not, they'll likely let you know if you get out of line. That's the whole point of this exercise. It would help to have a dialogue with a mentor, though, so that you can get some feedback and even learn about their own particular struggles with setting and maintaining limits.

What Boundaries Are Not

We can say what we need to say. We can gently, but assertively, speak our mind. We do not need to be judgmental, tactless, blaming or cruel when we speak our truths. - Melody Beattie

We went through some common misconceptions about boundaries in an earlier chapter and one of the most important things to understand about boundaries is that they are for your benefit and no one else's. Many are of the mistaken idea that, by stating their boundaries, they will finally be able to get people to behave the way they want them to. If this is your thinking, I suggest that you immediately step over to the nearest Al-Anon room for a change in perspective. Aside from not being a form of manipulation and control, here are some other things that boundaries are NOT:

Boundaries are not something that makes you unhappy. So many of us are scared to set boundaries, worried we won't be liked and our life will then be miserable. The reverse tends to be true. If you set boundaries, you then attract people who are willing to respect you and want good things for you.

Boundaries are not to limit your joy, but to protect your joy and your new-found serenity. Your relationships get better, and you actually enjoy the things you choose to do because they match your values.

Boundaries are not set in stone. As you learn more of who you are and experience personal lessons in life, you will change. So ,too, will your boundaries and we discuss this further in an upcoming chapter.

Boundaries are not about right or wrong. Your personal healthy boundaries are based on your own value system and perspective, and might be totally different than someone else's. This also means that you don't have to explain or defend your boundaries. You just need to set them. If someone doesn't want to abide by them or refuses to accept them, then question if you really need that person in your life anymore.

Enforcing Your Boundaries

Good fences make good neighbors. - Robert Frost

Recognizing that you need boundaries and setting limits in a healthy manner are just the beginning. While some people will be perfectly happy to respect your boundaries, many won't and this is where the real test begins. When you set boundaries, you might be tested, especially by those accustomed to controlling you, abusing you, or manipulating you. Plan on it, expect it, but be firm. Remember, your behavior must match the boundaries you are setting. You cannot establish a clear boundary successfully if you send a mixed message by apologizing for doing so or failing to enforce that boundary once it's set. Be firm, clear, and respectful.

Boundary Violations

People who violate your boundaries are
thieves. They steal time that doesn't belong to
them. – Elizabeth Grace Saunders

When someone violates your physical or emotional boundaries without your permission, you feel uncomfortable perhaps even threatened. When someone trespasses your boundaries by thoughtless or intrusive actions these actions are called... boundary violations. There are TWO types of boundary violations: violations of intrusion and violations of emotional   distance   -

1. **Violations of Intrusion** happen when a person is verbally, emotionally,   sexually   or   physically   abused   or   enmeshed.

2. **Violations of Emotional Distance** occur when emotional intimacy is less than what is appropriate for the relationship. Emotional distance is harmful, especially with children. A child has the right to expect closeness and emotional intimacy from her caretakers, and when it is excessively removed or cut off, it hurts and it becomes emotionally harmful. For example, when you were a child, if your parents only talked to you to give you orders or to reprimand you, this would be a violation of emotional distance. Children and adults need hugs, affection and emotional intimacy from their parents in order to feel safe   and   secure.

Violations of Emotional Distance are often difficult to validate because these wounds were caused by 'what wasn't done to you'. When you were a child, you did not have the power or wisdom to stop others from transgressing your boundaries. Adults could do as they wished with you because you were powerless to stop them. Now that you are an adult, you are able to use your adult powers to set mature, functional boundaries so that you can feel safe, sane and secure in the world.

Often when a child's boundaries are violated it is allowed to continue because the child has not been taught that he/she has the right to say "NO" when his/her boundaries have been breached. If you were not given permission as a child to say NO to protect your boundaries then you'll need to practice doing this as an adult.

Signs of Ignored Boundaries

You can tell boundaries are being ignored if there are one or more of the following characteristic symptoms.

- **Over Enmeshment** - This symptom requires everyone to follow the rule that everyone must do everything together and that everyone is to think, feel, and act in the same way. No one is allowed to deviate from the family or group norms. Everyone looks homogeneous. Uniqueness, autonomy and idiosyncratic behaviors are viewed as deviations from the norm.

- **Disassociation** - This symptom involves blanking out during a stressful emotional event. You feel your physical and/or emotional space being violated and you tell yourself something like: ``It doesn't matter." "Ignore it and it will go away soon enough." "No sense in fighting it, just hang on and it will be over soon." "Don't put up a struggle or else it will be worse for you." This blanking out results in your being out of touch with your feelings about what happened. It also may result in your inability to remember what happened.

- **Excessive Detachment** - This symptom occurs when neither you nor anyone else in the group or family is able to establish any fusion of emotions or affiliation of feelings. Everyone is totally independent from everyone else and there doesn't seem to be anything to hold you and them together in healthy union. You and they seem to lack a common purpose, goal, identity, or rationale for existing together. There is a seeming lack of desire from you and the other members to draw together to form a union because you fear loss of personal identity.

- **Victimhood or Martyrdom** - In this symptom, you identify yourself as a violated victim and become overly defensive to ward off further violation. Or it can be that once you accept your victimization you continue to be knowingly victimized and then let others know of your martyrdom.

- **Chip on the Shoulder** - This symptom is reflected in your interactions with others. Because of your anger over past violation of your emotional and/or physical space and the real or perceived ignoring of your rights by others, you have a "chip on your shoulder" that declares "I dare you to come too close!"

- **Invisibility** - This symptom involves your pulling in or over controlling so that others, even yourself, never know how you are really feeling or what you are really thinking. Your goal is not to be seen or heard so that your boundaries are not violated.

- **Aloofness or Shyness** - This symptom is a result of your insecurity from real or perceived experiences of being ignored or rejected in the past. This feels like a violation of your efforts to expand or stretch your boundaries to include others in your space. Once rejected you take the defensive posture to reject others before they reject you. This keeps you inward and unwilling or fearful of opening up your space to others.

- **Cold and Distant** - This symptom builds walls or barriers to insure that others do not permeate or invade your emotional or physical space. This too can be a defense, due to previous hurt and pain, from being violated, hurt, ignored or rejected. This stance is your declaration that "I've drawn the line over which I dare you to cross." It is a way to keep others out and put them off.

- **Smothering** - This symptom results when another is overly solicitous of your needs and interests. This cloying interest is overly intrusive into your emotional and physical space. It can be so overwhelming that you feel like you are being strangled, held too tightly and lack freedom to breathe on your own. You feel violated, used, and overwhelmed.

- **Lack of Privacy** - This symptom is present when you feel that nothing you think, feel, or do is your own business. You are expected to report to others in your family or group all the detail and content of your feelings, reactions, opinions, relationships and dealings with the outside world. You begin to feel that nothing you experience can be kept in the privacy of your own domain. You begin to believe you don't have a private domain or your own space into which you can escape to be your own person.

Emotional Abuse

There is a pretty fine line between issues of boundary violations and what we would term emotional abuse. Emotional abuse can take place in intimate relationships, in friendships, between parents and children, and even at work. Emotional abuse is elusive. Unlike physical abuse, the people doing it and receiving it may not even know it's happening. Emotional abuse symptoms vary but can invade any part of a person's life. Signs of emotional abuse include:

- Yelling or swearing
- Name calling or insults; mocking
- Threats and intimidation
- Ignoring or excluding
- Isolating
- Humiliating
- Denial of the abuse and blaming of the victim

Emotional abuse, like other types of abuse, tends to take the form of a cycle. In a relationship, this cycle starts when one partner emotionally abuses the other, typically to show dominance. The abuser then feels guilt, but not about what he (or she) has done, but more over the consequences of his actions. The abuser then makes up excuses for his own behavior to avoid taking responsibility over what has happened. The abuser then resumes "normal" behavior as if the abuse never happened and may, in fact, be extra charming, apologetic and giving – making the abused party believe that the abuser is sorry. The abuser then begins to fantasize about abusing his partner again and sets up a situation in which more emotional abuse can take place. In some countries emotional abuse is defined and the following examples of emotional abuse are given by *Justice Canada*:

- Threats of violence or abandonment

- Intentionally frightening
- Making an individual fear that they will not receive the food or care they need
- Lying
- Failing to check allegations of abuse against them
- Making derogative or slanderous statements about an individual to others
- Socially isolating an individual, failing to let them have visitors
- Withholding important information
- Demeaning an individual because of the language they speak
- Intentionally misinterpreting traditional practices
- Repeatedly raising the issue of death
- Telling an individual that they are too much trouble
- Ignoring or excessively criticizing
- Being over-familiar and disrespectful
- Unreasonably ordering an individual around; treating an individual like a servant or child

A more sophisticated form of psychological abuse is often referred to as "gaslighting." This happens when false information is presented with the intent of making victims doubt their own memory, perception, and sanity. Examples may range simply from the abuser denying that previous abusive incidents ever occurred to staging bizarre events with the intention of confusing the victim. It is important to remember is that emotional abuse is absolutely not your fault yet this is much more than a boundary issue. Abusers are expert manipulators with a knack for getting you to believe that the way you are being treated is your fault. These people know that everyone has insecurities, and they use those insecurities against you. Abusers can convince you that you do not deserve better treatment or that they are treating you this way to "help" you. Some abusers even act quite charming and nice in public so that others have a good impression of them. In private is a different story, which is also quite baffling.

Alex:

Gaslighting takes effect in several forms and lately I have been experiencing intense feelings of self-doubt, anxiety and feeling like I'm crazy or out of touch with reality. Basically when one party can't take responsibility for their actions, be open, kind or loving when a relationship is challenged it's easier to pull away and suggest that the reaction and actions of the other trying to communicate or reach a resolution are crazy. I've know about this concept for a while and I can now see that it's not my fault, I am not out of touch with reality or overreacting. It is easier for someone to treat me as if I am rather than take responsibility for their actions.

If you see yourself in these words, know that there is little hope for your relationship to improve. It would take a monumental amount of insight and motivation for the abuser to change and unfortunately, this is rarely the case. If you are in an abusive relationship, I urge you to get out (the ultimate boundary) and seek professional help if needed. Often the first step in leaving the abuser is obtaining counseling just to rebuild your self-esteem so that you can leave. I particularly want you to know that you may "love" this person, but that they do not "love" you or respect you. I assure you that in time you will get over this person if you break it off. You will be making the right decision...no looking back.

Honoring and Enforcing Your Boundaries

Honoring your own boundaries is the clearest message to others to honor them, too. – Gina Greenlee

Now that we know what boundary violations and ignored boundaries look like from every conceivable angle, what can you do about it? Enforcing a boundary assumes that you have defined a behavior that is unacceptable to you, have kindly let the other person know how you feel, and have given the consequence or alternative behavior that you'd prefer. If the behavior continues, this means that the other person either didn't understand, didn't care, or needs some reinforcement of the notion that you really do mean what you're saying. There are several approaches to enforcing boundaries that get progressively more firm.

How to Enforce Boundaries and Still Have Friends

Yes. it is possible, but you'll want to be big about how you handle this. Following are tips and phrasing examples of how to do this.

1. **Respond immediately** at the first sense that the other person is about to get near or cross your boundary. If you wait, you are playing a hopeful or victim game. Do not be a DQ (drama queen). Stop the disturbances before they happen - and most are predictable if you'll make the commitment to take care of yourself.

2. **Be constructive at first**. You can protect yourself and at the same time make this a contribution to the other person. You needn't get on your high horse and do the "you offended me" routine. Say things like:

• As I said before, I am particularly sensitive about people raising their voice to me. Would you be willing to speak quietly with me?

• Yes, I will send you that article you need, but may I ask a favor of you sometime?

• We've discussed this in the past. I am unable to be with you when you are angry and I'm going to leave the room when you are disturbed. I do want to spend time with you and I love you.

The Sledgehammer Approach

Have you ever refused a request, pretty clearly, you thought, and yet had to deal with the person in question coming back with "But, but, but?" If so, maybe you gave in, just this once, just to get the person to stop bugging you. But maybe later the pit of your stomach informed you that doing so was the wrong thing, and you felt violated. Sometimes the other person seems unable to hear your unconditionally constructive request to back off. Assuming you are willing to put yourself first, here are a couple of straight-shooting ways to protect your boundaries. And you may lose the friendship or relationship.

• Joe, it's not ok for you to speak to me that way. If it happens again, I will have to walk away from this relationship.

• I am no longer willing to help you, if you keep fighting me.

• Karen, I cannot hear one more word about how badly Michael treated you.

• Susie, I can no longer spend any more time with you, because you are insensitive about things that matter a great deal to me.

• Bill, you may not be late anymore for work. Next time, you're fired.

If you're getting fed up with someone, first look to see where you didn't act early enough. Then, make the biggest request you can of that person to have them treat you exactly as you wish and need to be treated. Especially in personal relationships: DO NOT try to figure out whether they can do what you're asking. Just ask for or demand it. If they care enough, they will accept it and change their behavior accordingly. If they give you a bad time about it or can't seem to deliver, then it is time to get this need met by someone else, or to let go of the relationship until such time as they are able to be good to you.

Terry:

Yes, the trick was not in getting other people to honor my boundaries. The trick was learning how to honor them myself. I've struggled tremendously with boundaries. I'm still learning how to create and honor the intricate boundaries most people don't think about. I'm similar in that I don't communicate my needs/feelings/boundaries and in many cases people do honor them if they know them. I think healthy people make those small communications without much thought.

Honoring Others Boundaries

*Boundaries represent awareness, knowing
what the limits are and then respecting those
limits. – David W. Earle*

It would seem to make sense that, if we expect others to respect our new-found healthy boundaries, we'd be willing to start respecting the boundaries of others as well. By establishing boundaries that honor you , you set limits on how people can treat you or act around you and thus reduce or eliminate the hurt and annoyances they can be causing you. By honoring the boundaries established by others, we are giving them that same consideration.

There are many hang-ups that those in recovery can get tangled in that are not conducive to growth. While we may want to cushion the fall for each other, this is not always the best way. By being overly sympathetic toward others we enable them to continue their harmful behavior. This not only disempowers them, it adversely affects you. Sometimes we just really need to mind our own business! We have enough stuff of our own to deal with; we don't need someone else's drama. We are all here to enjoy our sober experience, explore possibilities, and develop our own soul. When we carry burdens for someone else, we rob them of the experience to learn specific lessons their soul has arranged.

If someone close has asked for some space or time apart from you, honor their request. We don't have to be entertained or always together in order to have a healthy relationship. If your partner or friend needs space, you don't have to feel as though they don't like you or don't want to be with you. They may simply need a break from your energy - especially if you are carrying a negative charge and are not attempting to clear it. Give your loved one a chance to recover and recharge their batteries. Why not spend the time engaging in your own spiritual work? It can only make your relationship better.

Now, when you feel that a close friend (in recovery or not) may be in real trouble, this is a different story. We often have to trust our guts and know when it is ok to intervene and try to help someone else who is suffering. Having lost friends and loved ones over the years to this disease, I know how painful it is and what a slippery slope it can be. There is sometimes a fine line between helping someone up who has fallen and chasing someone down. With time and the help of others in the program, we are able to make these difficult choices.

People's personal space boundaries vary a great deal. Even when we do not make contact, if we get very close to someone, especially in the context of differences of opinion, that person may feel intimidated. The relationship between intention and impact can be very helpful to consider in such circumstances. Our intention may be to signal connection, interest, or enthusiasm. The other person may feel uncomfortable, invaded, or trapped. I know that hugging is a big thing in recovery circles. Frankly, some people don't like it and we often make too many assumptions about this with regards to the wants and needs of others.

If you honor and respect yourself, and treat others with the same dignity you would want to be treated with, your whole life will change for the better. From this day forward, promise to assert yourself, take a stand for your personal freedom, and never intentionally encroach on someone else's boundaries again.

Boundaries in Relationships

Individuals set boundaries to feel safe,
respected, and heard. - Pamela Cummins

Addiction and healthy relationships are mutually exclusive things. This means that these two cannot exist at the same time. Some of us may have been under the delusion when we came into recovery that the only thing that needed fixing was the fact that we drank too much or couldn't stop taking drugs. A little time and some soul searching generally proves this notion wrong. In fact, when I looked back upon a series of broken and tattered relationships, it didn't take a rocket scientist to figure out what the common denominator was. Recognizing that I was likely the problem wasn't enough to solve it, though. It has taken many years of even more growth and discovery to approach the person that I want to be in relationships, and there is still work to be done. Whether branded by our upbringing as to what is acceptable or warped by years of chemical abuse and dangerous living, it's pretty clear that old ideas about boundaries in intimate relationships, family dynamics, and even boundaries with our children need examining when we come into recovery.

Boundaries in Recovery

Boundaries in Intimate Relationships

The person you're meant to be with will never have to be chased, begged, or given an ultimatum. - Mandy Hale

Those suffering from addiction often have many negative relationships when they enter recovery. Many times these unhealthy or negative relationships spawn from unhealthy boundaries. These unhealthy boundaries that were present in addiction include either giving too much or taking too much from another person. The individual may have put other's needs before their own needs, or put their needs above others in their lives.

Learning when to say no, and establishing boundaries, helps those in recovery to eliminate relationship issues that could potentially manifest into an excuse to use or relapse into old behaviors. Most of us had dramatic relationships and circumstances in our past lives, and eliminating these behaviors and old ideas helps us to focus solely on recovery and moving forward.

There is sound reasoning behind the suggestion in many programs that people who are newly sober avoid getting involved in new romantic relationships for a period of time. While many of us ignore these suggestions to our detriment, it soon becomes clear that one or both parties involved has some serious boundary issues that still need to be identified and resolved. Either we get entirely too serious too quick, or we put up walls and end up alienating others. It soon becomes clear that the practice of establishing healthy boundaries in intimate relationships is of the utmost importance to success in recovery and, overall, to emotional sobriety.

Boundaries in Recovery

Boundaries can be problematic in intimate relationships if they are too close or they are too distant. The following two lists will point out the differences and why both of these circumstances can be difficult for those involved in these types of relationships.

When boundaries are too close (when they are enmeshed or when one person lets the other in too much), you might:

- have a hard time saying no
- give in too much
- get involved too quickly
- trust too easily
- intrude on others (such as violate their boundaries)
- stay in relationships too long

When boundaries are too distance (not letting people in enough, detached), you might:

- have difficulty saying yes in a relationship
- isolate yourself
- distrust too easily
- feel lonely
- stay in relationships too briefly

As some of us show up with almost no idea about what love really is, here is a great basic list to put things into perspective:

Love Is…

- Responsibility
- Hard Work
- Pleasure
- Commitment
- Caring
- Honesty
- Trust
- Communication
- Sharing
- Negotiating
- Compromising

- Openness
- Respect
- Appreciating Differences
- Vulnerability
- Friendship
- Strong Feelings
- Helping Your Partner
- Helping Yourself

Love Is Not...

- Jealousy
- Pain
- Sex
- Being Selfish
- Getting Pregnant to Keep the Relationship
- Dependency
- Intimidation
- Fear
- Manipulation
- Expecting All Your Needs To Be Met
- Possessiveness
- Violence
- Obsession
- Cruelty
- Making Someone Pregnant to Keep the Relationship
- Giving Up Yourself
- Scoring
- Proving Yourself
- Lies
- Controlling

A successful relationship is composed of two individuals - each with a clearly defined sense of her or his own identity. Without our own understanding of self, of who we are and what makes us unique, it is difficult to engage in the process of an ongoing relationship in a way that functions smoothly and enhances each of the partners. I don't know about you but I had no sense of self when I first got sober. None! I was propelled by self-will but this isn't the same thing. We need a sense of self in order to clearly communicate our needs and desires to our partner.

When we have a strong conception of our own identity, we can appreciate and love those qualities in our partner that make him or her a unique person. I don't know anyone who developed such a conception overnight, or even in just a few years. This takes time. When two people come together, each with a clear definition of her or his own individuality, the potential for intimacy and commitment can be astounding. The similarities between two people may bring them together, but their differences contribute to the growth, excitement and mystery of their relationship.

One feature of a healthy sense of self is the way we understand and work with boundaries. Personal boundaries are the limits we set in intimate relationships that allow us to protect ourselves. Boundaries come from having a good sense of our own self-worth. They make it possible for us to separate our own thoughts and feelings from those of others and to take responsibility for what we think, feel and do. Boundaries allow us to rejoice in our own uniqueness. Good boundaries protect us from abuse and pave the way to achieving true intimacy. They help us take care of ourselves and this may be a welcome change for someone in recovery.

Lack of a Sense of Identity

When we lack a sense of our own identity and the boundaries which protect us, we tend to draw our identities from our partner. We can't imagine who we would be without our relationship. We become willing to do anything it takes to make the relationship work, even if it means giving up our emotional security, friends, integrity, sense of self-respect, independence, or job. We may endure physical, emotional or sexual abuse just to save the relationship.

The more rational alternative is to find out who we are and what makes us unique - and to rejoice in this discovery. Realize that your value and worth as a person are not necessarily dependent on having a significant other in your life, that you can function well as an independent person in your own right. When you move into accepting yourself, your relationships will actually have a chance to grow and flourish. This journey of self-discovery can be challenging - but highly rewarding. Working with a trained therapist can provide the structure and support needed to take on this task.

Below are some of the ways in which unhealthy boundaries may show themselves in intimate relationships and the healthier alternatives:

Settling for Second Best

We may cling to the irrational belief that things are good enough in the relationship - that we feel a measure of security and that this is as good as it's likely to get. In the process, however, we give up the chance to explore our sense of fulfillment in life. We give up our own life dreams in order to maintain the security of a relationship. There is a feeling that if one of the partners grows and finds personal life fulfillment, the relationship would be damaged.

A healthy relationship is one in which our boundaries are strong enough, yet flexible enough, to allow us to flourish with our own uniqueness. There is a sense of respect on the part of both partners that allows each to live as full a life as possible and to explore their own personal potential. We don't have to give up ourselves for a relationship. Healthy boundaries allow trust and security to develop in a relationship.

Over-Responsibility and Guilt

One characteristic of growing up in a dysfunctional household is that we may learn to feel guilty if we fail to ensure the success and happiness of other members of the household. Thus, in adulthood, we may come to feel responsible for our partner's failures. The guilt we feel when our partner fails may drive us to keep tearing down our personal boundaries so that we are always available to the other person. When we feel overly responsible for another person's life experiences, we deprive them of one of the most important features of an independent, healthy and mature life - the ability to make our own life choices and accept the consequences of our decisions.

A healthier response is to show our partners respect by allowing them to succeed or fail on their own terms. You, of course, can be there to comfort your partner when times become difficult, and you can rejoice together when success is the outcome. When boundaries are healthy, you are able to say, "I trust and respect you to make your own life choices. As my equal partner, I will not try to control you by taking away your choices in life."

The Difference Between Love and Rescue

People who grow up in a dysfunctional family may fail to learn the difference between love and sympathy. Children growing up in these conditions may learn to have sympathy for the emotional crippling in their parents' lives and feel that the only time they get attention is when they show compassion for the parent. They feel that when they forgive, they are showing love. Actually, they are rescuing the parent and enabling abusive behavior to continue. They learn to give up their own protective boundaries in order to take care of the dysfunctioning parent.

In adulthood, they carry these learned behaviors into their relationships. If they can rescue their partner, they feel that they are showing love. They get a warm, caring, sharing feeling from helping their partner - a feeling they call love. But this may actually encourage their partner to become needy and helpless. An imbalance can then occur in the relationship in which one partner becomes the rescuer and the other plays the role of the helpless victim. In this case, healthy boundaries which allow both partners to live complete lives are absent. Mature love requires the presence of healthy and flexible boundaries.

Sympathy and compassion are worthy qualities, but they are not to be confused with love, especially when boundaries have become distorted. Healthy boundaries lead to respect for the other and equality in a relationship, an appreciation for the aliveness and strength of the other person, and a mutual flow of feelings between the two partners - all features of mature love. When one partner is in control and the other is needy and helpless, there is no room for the normal give-and-take of a healthy relationship.

Fantasy vs. Reality

Children from dysfunctional households often feel that things will get better someday, that a normal life may lie in the future. Indeed, some days things are fairly normal, but then the bad times return again. It's the normal days that encourage the fantasy that all problems in the family might someday be solved. How many times in your addiction did you delude yourself into thinking that "this time it would be different" or that a certain circumstance would produce a different outcome? I know that I was a master at this sort of thing and I was living in a fantasy world. It's the same idea here.

When they grow up, these adults carry the same types of fantasy into their relationships. They may portray to others the myth that they have the perfect relationship - and they may believe, to themselves, that someday all of their relationship problems will somehow be solved. They ignore the abuse, manipulation, imbalance and control in the relationship. By ignoring the problems, they are unable to confront them - and the fantasy of a happier future never comes to pass. Unhealthy boundaries, where we collude with our partner in believing the myth that everything is fine, make it difficult to come to terms with the troubles of the relationship.

We've already talked about how to set limits in the last chapter. The key to doing this with intimate relationships is to do it early and to be kind. If you delay too long, you'll build up resentment, which isn't fair to you or the person you care about, and will only make the conversation harder. One of the biggest mistakes people often make (I did this for years) is assuming their loved ones can read their minds. This (usually) isn't the case, and rather than requiring that the people you care about "just know" what you need, you have to tell them, also taking into account their wants and needs.

It's interesting to note that relationships with too close or too distant boundaries are actually attempts at self-love. For instance, when someone behaves very closely in relationships, he or she is attempting to win the other person over. That person is often unconsciously looking for the acceptance and love of the other person. However, what often happens as a result is the other person in the relationship exploits or takes advantage of it. On the other hand, when someone isolates themselves in a relationship and the relationship becomes too distant, he or she might be trying to protect themselves but then they do not end up receiving the support they need in a relationship.

However, healthy boundaries can keep you safe. For instance, saying no in relationships that are too close can protect you from unsafe sex, using substances if your partner invites you to do so, abusive relationships, and giving in to unfair demands. Meanwhile, saying yes in relationships that are too distant might allow you to rely on others, let yourself be known in relationships, and help yourself feel supported. Boundaries can be set within any aspect of life and can establish limitation upon how much you need in a relationship. Learning how to have healthy boundaries can create relationships that are long lasting, healthy, and fulfilling.

Lora:

I hurt my boyfriend's feelings last month when I told him I needed time to myself to study for a test and get more solid sleep so I can excel more in the employment arena. He got over it, but it was still difficult to say it. It's definitely tricky to balance your own needs and goals with someone's desire to always be around you. I tend to feel a bit suffocated when someone wants me around ALL THE TIME. But we're finding ways to each have our own time. Being honest and communicating clearly are probably the most helpful thing, I've found.

Boundaries With Family

Being able to say No is a necessary ingredient
in a healthy lifestyle. – David W. Earle

As boundaries are initially learned and developed from our interactions with family when we are very young, it's no surprise that changing this dynamic later in life seems next to impossible. If you remember that boundaries are for you, though, and not anyone else the goal may appear more within reach. As adults, we learn that it's ok to challenge many of those both spoken and unspoken rules that we grew up with that may no longer be serving our greater good. An example of a rule and a boundary learned from your family might be the directive, "we don't talk about mom getting drunk and passing out on the floor to people outside the family".

Alcoholic families tend to have rigid or enmeshed boundaries, which severely limits communication between family members or others. Rigid boundaries tend to be associated with disengaged families, where members are very psychologically distant from one another. On the other extreme are the enmeshed families, where boundaries are blurred and unclear. Enmeshment involves an unhealthy amount of closeness and intensity between family members. The two extremes, disengaged or enmeshed family systems lead to major "boundary issues" in adult relationships. Disengaged families with rigid boundaries make it difficult for family members to allow others to get close to them. Enmeshed families, with weak boundaries, tend to create a tendency toward over-involvement with others, and the sense of losing one's own identity in the process. Alcoholic families also have some tendency to move back and forth between enmeshment and disengagement as they move in and out of crises.

I can't count the number of conversations that I have had over the years with friends in recovery who are continually frustrated that their family of origin is not giving them what they feel they need and deserve. Their mother is selfish, father won't stop drinking, siblings are rude and condescending, ad infinitum. While sad that we don't always get what we need from our families, this isn't surprising and we learn in recovery that one of the true pathways to peace is to stop trying to change people to suit our wants and needs. For anyone who hasn't heard The Serenity Prayer recently, here it is:

God, grant me the serenity to accept the things I cannot change, the courage to change the things I can, and the wisdom to know the difference.

There's nothing like family to either bring out the people pleaser or the inner child in you. They know how to push your buttons because they installed them. You share the longest history with them than with anyone else and often end up assuming roles that aren't healthy and that don't serve you, especially in recovery. Families can manifest dysfunction in various ways. They might have difficulty communicating without yelling or might show disrespect and passive-aggressive behaviors. Boundary issues present in these types of families in different forms. They might be apathetic toward one another and under-involved or, at the other end of the spectrum, overly involved to the point where individuals lose their identities. Establishing rules regarding boundaries is a good first step in creating healthier family dynamics.

As that Serenity Prayers teaches us (I recite it often), the only thing that we really have control over is ourselves and our attitudes. Our families are going to respond to us and our boundaries however they wish and experience has taught me that expecting anything in particular from someone, such as praise or a particular behavior, is futile. It's best to just live life in a manner that is healthiest for you, so here are a few tips for dealing with family members and boundaries:

Expect that it will be a process of trial and error for you. Learn as you go, don't expect to get it 'right' first time or even the fifth or fifteenth time but do realize that you will gradually see progress over time although you might not recognize it at the time.

It's best to start off with known factors – it's amazing how many people act 'surprised' about stuff that's been going on for ages. You know exactly where, which and how family members tend to jump or rattle your fence – work out the best alternative response for you.

I worked out several years ago after a stern talking to from a close friend about holding myself hostage on phone calls, that I didn't need to say "My boundary is that I don't want to spend two hours on the phone with you draining the sh*t out of me each day"; Instead, I just needed to show it by having shorter calls, having opt out reasons ready, and saying something as simple as "I can't talk right now". The sky did not fall down.

Some people if given an inch will take a mile. Or they'll at least try. Just because someone takes the chance and asks, doesn't mean that asking equals you must acquiesce. Remember - "No" is a complete sentence.

They can and will try the guilt card but it's best to stick to the facts. I appreciate that I came out of my mother's womb or that somebody else did something for me, but that doesn't mean that I owe boundary busts. When you put boundaries in place that weren't there before, expect some push back, guilt trips and even extreme anger in some circumstances. Don't apologize or explain, just be firm - over and over again.

Stop trying to control outcomes. Let the chips fall where they may. I used to think that I was the supreme puppet master when, in reality, I was just pissing people off and continually scheming to get my way. Simply stating my wants and needs without regard to the outcome is a much simpler way to live. Yes, some will get their backs up and I have gone through a grieving process of sorts – people are going to say what they're going to say, think what they're going to think and do what they're going to do, so it's best to get on with the business of being you.

If you want to do a favor and can do it, plus it doesn't involve you eroding your self-esteem, knock yourself out. I like doing things for my mother for instance; what I don't like is being harangued or guilted into something by anybody including myself. If you're being asked to do something that goes against your own values or is even illegal, decline and don't feel guilty about it. Yes of course you can go and rob a shop if asked but does it mean you should say yes?

Michelle:

I am a 40+ year old woman, who has a father that would text me multiple times a day and get angry at me when I did not get back to him stat. Today, I told him that as an adult, he needs to respect my boundaries and realize that I am not available to get back to him when he wants. I told him that I wouldn't mind keeping in touch with him once a week. He didn't handle this well. He started texting insults to me.

I simply responded back that I wasn't offended by what he said and that I was speaking the truth and I am sorry that he could not handle that. I believe that my father is very toxic. I will not tolerate his nasty behavior.

One major goal in recovery is to develop healthy boundaries. Healthy families have boundaries that allow each family member to feel confident in their assessment of reality. Healthy family boundaries clearly define appropriate roles, responsibilities, and acceptable behavior. Boundaries don't shift according to the mood of the most powerful person in the family. Healthy family boundaries encourage self-sufficiency, freedom to disclose feelings, wants, and needs. Healthy boundaries are reliable and consistent over time but are flexible enough to change as family circumstances and membership changes. Healthy boundaries allow each person to take care of their own individual needs and responsibilities while maintaining an appropriate level of connection/closeness to others.

Recovery is a challenging time, regardless of whether you are the recovering addict or a family member. A casualty in the family dynamics of addiction can be the development of unhealthy boundaries or a loss of boundaries. One of the tasks of recovery for everyone is to develop healthy boundaries. Sometimes people in recovery have to learn or re-learn what the appropriate roles and codes of behavior are for various family members and for others outside of the family. It involves defining and describing that personal space and sense of appropriate treatment by others. It also involves defining appropriate treatment of others. An example could be the family member who gives frequent unsolicited advice, with the expectation that you will follow that advice. Setting the boundaries with this family member might involve telling them that you don't want or need their advice or thanking them for their concern, while saying that you will be making a decision by weighing the merits of your own pros and cons.

Boundaries in Recovery

With a healthy sense of personal boundaries, we begin to listen to and trust ourselves and others. We do not have to accept blame or unreasonable responsibility from others. With a healthy sense of boundaries, you can believe that you deserve to be treated with dignity and respect, that your wants, needs, and preferences are important, that you have personal rights, and that you have responsibility for self. As your sense of boundaries become clearer to you, they will become clearer to others. You will also be able to communicate those boundaries to others without acting out feelings. Appropriate boundaries and a clear sense of self allow us to get close to others without fear of rejection or engulfment.

Boundaries With Children

Guilt can prevent us from setting the boundaries that would be in our best interests, and in other people's best interests. - Melody Beattie

In many parts of this book, we talk about the way that our ideas about boundaries were formed when we were very young and, perhaps, the need when we get sober to re-think some of those old ideas that may not be serving our greatest good. What happens when we get sober and find that we may have been the ones who, through our warped thinking and unhealthy living, have instilled some of those same sorts of ideas in our own children? This is very common as are the feelings of guilt and remorse that surface once we "wake up" and realize all of the things that we had been missing with our precious children.

Boundaries with children, no matter what the age, are difficult at best. When you change the rules mid-stream expect that there will be an adjustment period. Children many not fully trust that the new, sober, parent is there to stay and there could be a great deal of resentment present. On the other hand, everyone may be just so relieved and happy that the nightmare is finally over that all rules take a backseat for a period of time. Regardless of which way this pendulum swings, it's going to need to settle back into some semblance of balance at some point - for everyone's sake.

As far as limits go, you can think of a boundary as the line you draw around yourself to define where you end and where your child begins. This isn't always easy. And let's face it, kids push the boundaries every day, all the time. They are wired to test us and see how far they can go; it's in their nature. As parents, we sometimes cross boundaries ourselves in our attempts to fix things for them. Understand that one of our most important jobs as parents is to stay loving and separate from our children. We do this by clearly defining our principles, staying in our role as a parent, and sticking to our bottom lines.

How do you know if you might be blurring boundaries as a parent? Here are some signs:

- Doing for your child what he can (or should) do for himself.
- Constantly asking questions; interrogating your child over everything.
- Letting your child invade your boundaries as a couple—making your kids the center focus at all times.
- Over-sharing with your child about your life; treating them like a friend rather than your child.
- Giving up your parental authority and allowing your child to take control of the household.
- Living through your child vicariously; feeling as if their achievements are yours, and their failures are yours as well.
- Your child is upset, and you fall apart.

I know that I exhibited many of these signs both before I got sober and after. My son was a toddler when I got sober and I was completely enmeshed with him. When I was still drinking, I would fall apart when he was unhappy and my well-being was very much tied to his moods. Not much changed after I got sober for quite some time. I still spoiled him, mainly due to guilt, and he was a large part of my focus aside from my program. Slowly, I was able to change this and our relationship now, many years later, is much healthier. He has his own life, with his own hardships, yet feels safe talking to me about most things.

Parents in recovery often need to get back to the basics of providing a secure and stable environment for their kids. In particular, parents are responsible for setting boundaries in the household, in order to foster an environment where their children can be heard, but also encouraged to develop patience, self-awareness, and so on. Here are four reasons why parents need to be "in charge" of boundary-setting in order to set the tone for a child's emotional development:

1. Parental boundaries allow kids to feel safe.

Secure boundaries set by the parent (not negotiated by the child) reduce anxiety. Rules and routines like meal times, bed times, homework time, and screen time — that are set and monitored by the parent — create predictability in a child's life. Predictability reduces uncertainty, and that reduces anxiety.

Parents should not value a child's self-expression over a child's sense of security. Setting boundaries doesn't make you a mean or unfair parent, even if your child says that to you at the time, out of anger. When a child tries to negotiate a later bed time this comes at a cost of the child's sense of security because it allows the child to feel he or she has more power than the adult.

2. Children have undeveloped prefrontal lobes.

In other words, a child's brain is not fully developed, and hence shouldn't be given decision-making power over adults. According to Child Developmental Psychologist Piaget, "magical thinking" predominates in children aged two to seven. This "magical thinking" is what makes children amazing and so full of wonder. But it also suggests that young children are not equipped to be in charge of big decisions — beyond choosing peanut butter and jelly or grilled cheese.

School-aged children from eight to eleven years of age are largely concrete in their thinking. This is why elementary kids love rules and often like the world to be black and white. After all, structure ensures predictability and security. It is only after age 12 that children begin to develop more abstract and nuanced thinking. This is why adolescence is a more appropriate time to experiment with rules and limits. Yet parents still need to be "in charge" of setting boundaries with their teenage children, as they are still developing the prefrontal controls around impulsivity, decision making, and problem-solving (never mind all the hormonal shifts!).

Even as we know more about brain development, we seem to have become less attuned to thinking about our children's unique developmental stage, and what is an appropriate level of choice for them to have. Many parents today negotiate with their five year-olds as if they are mini-adults; thinking kids understand all the gradations of why rules change and shift.

3. Parental limits disrupt narcissism and entitlement.

For many families, a child's emotions, needs and desires can run the parent's whole day rather than the other way around. Narcissism is normal, and is developmentally appropriate in small children.

Yet unless the early-development narcissism is eventually disrupted, children continue to feel like the world revolves around them and become narcissistic adults. Parental boundaries allow children to grow up, to understand they can't always get their way, to be more patient and mature. Knowing that there is a limit to how much comfort and pleasure their parents will provide, children can learn to cope with disappointment; as an added bonus, the mild disappointment often brought about by boundaries can also help children to develop empathy - perhaps for others who have discomfort and disappointment. Understanding the meaning of "limits" allows kids to be more connected to the real world.

It's OK and perfectly appropriate for a parent's rationale to stop at this: "I am making this decision because I'm the parent, and you're the child." The notion of a parent being "in charge" is not a power-trip if done in a gentle but firm way to promote a child's feeling of safety and security.

4. We all learn from struggling a bit.

In any developmental task from walking to talking to learning to read or drive a car, kids need to struggle. Struggle is how we mature and learn mastery of new things. If children are brought up with the expectation that they will always be "in charge," they want things to be easy. They also parents to remove struggle and, fix their disappointments. A parent in charge knows it is not only OK for a child to struggle with a limit or a rule, it is actually good and healthy. It is OK if they have to turn off their video game to do their reading, or are asked to eat more vegetables or do an extra chore to help mom.

Parents who set boundaries are not trying to make their child happy in the moment (though sometimes they are!). Rather, more importantly, they are trying to have their child develop skills to successfully launch into the world at 18.

Now that we know why boundaries are a good idea with kids, let's take a look at how to start putting those in place. Good limitations imposed by parents involves making sure the boundaries are clear, and known, ahead of time.

1. Less is more:

Follow the guideline of a special education teacher we know. "Five rules respected 100% of the time are better than 20 rules with haphazard compliance."

2. Be precise:

Miscommunication is not the way to establish a positive environment. Effective communication works. It pays to make sure everyone is on the same page.

3. Involve the kids in the design:

Have a family pow-wow. Family communication gets everyone involved in designing the boundaries. When children share ownership of the rules, they're more invested.

4. Draw up a contract:

Once the "Family Ten-Commandments" have been established, write up a document that everyone will sign.

5. Post the rules:

Post copies of the contract in the kitchen and in each bedroom. Remember, these are not restrictions so much as rules by which to live.

6. Recognize appropriate behavior:

Teachers refer to this as, "Catch 'em when things are going well." Too many of us come down on violations like a ton of bricks and never pay attention to what's going well. If it's attention they're after, they'll get it one way or the other.

7. Avoid labeling children as "good" and "bad":

Children, and adults, behave in ways that are acceptable and in ways that are unacceptable. Labeling a child as "bad" will do little to improve behavior and a lot to create a negative self-image.

8. NEVER play Mom against Dad:

"Good-cop, bad-cop" is not a useful game at home. "Wait until your father gets home," suggests authority that's divided. Parents must have each other's backs. It's another way to be consistent. This can also lead to a very specific behavior known as triangulation.

Let's say that the parents have split up and that the two parents cease to want to talk to each other, and start to do their communicating through their child. Every time the child transfers to a parent's house, he or she is told to tell the other parent a bunch of information. Even worse, each parent may start putting the other parent down in front of the child, in the process, loading the child up with conflicting duties and emotions. The child may even be inappropriately asked to choose one parent over the other. This sort of communication through a child is an example of Triangulation, which is a common shape suggesting unhealthy boundaries are present. In this scenario, the child's emotional life is hijacked and invaded by his or her parent's unhealthy agendas, and the child suffers as a result.

9. Employ "natural consequences" when possible:

When raising teenagers, natural consequences just make more sense. For younger children, this helps associate negative outcomes with specific behavior. Examples of natural consequences are: Not paying allowance when chores aren't completed, letting a child face discipline at school for behavior, or not bailing them out of jail when arrested.

10. Be trustworthy:

Discipline based on trust is life enhancing. Training children seldom works in the absence of trust. So be true to your word. If you make a promise to your child, keep it. If you tell them there will be a punishment or consequence for not obeying, follow through.

Children need discipline in order to grow into responsible, caring and productive adults. Some parents believe that discipline is a way to control their child through punishment. However, it is important to know the root word of discipline is 'disciple' which means to lead and guide by example. Just as many of us got sober by following the actions of those who came before us and emulating the behaviors of other "sober" people, so too will our children do the same with what they see in the home. Children may not always seem as though they are listening, but they see everything you do. A parent's job is to instruct, train, educate and nurture your children as they go through the numerous developmental stages of childhood, and parenting by example gets more results than most realize.

I believe that inspiration and spiritual development is job #1 for parents. It is our personal growth that inspires our children. Children begin totally dependent upon us. Then adolescence deals with "tumultuous change" in the teenage brain as well as peer pressure. It requires our very best example and efforts to lead our children through this challenging period.

It is never too late to change our parenting. Our children learn from us at a far deeper level than our words. Children read our hearts, not our minds.

Shifting Boundaries

That which yields is not always weak. -
Jacqueline Carey

Alcoholics and addicts tend to be all or nothing people, many times even in recovery. One of the things that I had to learn when I got sober was to be a little bit more flexible and to try to see some of the grey areas, not just the black and white. Things don't always have to be good or bad, large or small, fast or slow, easy or hard. In fact, they can be neutral, medium, normal, average, or even just undetermined. The same holds true with boundaries. While we will want to defend a boundary once we have set it with someone, it's always ok to change our minds and shift those boundaries as situations, relationships, and we change.

There's a difference between healthy boundaries and rigid boundaries. You don't want to be a controlling or dictatorial person. That's not the goal. The goal is a healthy relationship with those close to you, balanced by a sense of understanding, mutual support, and give-and-take. There may be occasions when you choose to bend your boundaries or allow someone to cross the line. When someone is hurt or sad, needs extra support, asks for an exception with respect and kindness - these are times to show flexibility and love. As you gain confidence around your boundaries, you will know when and how to bend them.

You can also find persons who, knowing full well that they are being hurt, will sometimes set aside their boundaries as an act of charity for others. For example, if people push past you to get on a bus, you might decide to say nothing, knowing that people who would push past you to get on a bus will also react with hostility if you say anything to them about their rude behavior. In this case you can set aside your boundaries and tolerate their rude behavior with forbearance, praying that they might someday learn to act with charity to others. Yet these same persons who can willingly set aside their boundaries can just as well defend them. For example, if someone at work uses foul language, you can say that you do not like to hear such talk; if the talk persists, you can get up and walk away.

Boundaries need to be flexible, yet hold their shape. If, for example, we are interacting with a stranger, then it's important to have more rigidity in our boundary. Once we know the person and feel comfortable with them, it's important that our boundary become more flexible. Knowing when, and with whom, to do this is an example of being emotionally and mentally healthy. Also, give yourself permission to change your mind. Even the most prepared of us can be caught off guard and agree to something we later realize we didn't actually want to agree to. And many of us forget we are allowed to have second thoughts. So we feel even more violated because we said yes to something we wish we hadn't, and now we think we are stuck. But we aren't. All it takes is a sentence to reverse a decision you regret.

Sometimes, the boundaries that we set to protect ourselves could end up stifling some of that continued growth that emotional sobriety so requires. I go to a lot of meetings where I hear the phrase "peeling away the layers" thrown out. This is very applicable here. Consider the analogy of our continuing growth to that of a tree, instead of an onion. Trees grow up through their branches and down through their roots into the earth. They also grow wider with each passing year. As they do, they shed the bark that served to protect them but now is no longer big enough to contain them. In the same way, we create some boundaries and develop defenses to protect ourselves and then, at a certain point, we outgrow them. If we don't allow ourselves to shed our protective layer, we can't expand to our full potential.

Trees need their protective bark to enable the delicate process of growth and renewal to unfold without threat. Likewise, we need our boundaries and defenses so that the more vulnerable parts of ourselves can safely heal and unfold. But our growth also depends upon our ability to soften, loosen, and shed boundaries and defenses we no longer need. It is often the case in life that structures we put in place to help us grow eventually become constricting.

Unlike a tree, we must consciously decide when it's time to shed our bark and expand our boundaries, so we can move into our next ring of growth. Many spiritual teachers have suggested that our egos don't disappear so much as they become large enough to hold more than just our small sense of self - the boundary of self widens to contain people and beings other than just "me." Each time we shed a layer of defensiveness or ease up on a boundary that we no longer need, we metaphorically become bigger people. With this in mind, it is important that we take time to question our boundaries and defenses. While it is essential to set and honor the protective barriers we have put in place, it is equally important that we soften and release them when the time comes. In doing so, we create the space for our next phase of growth.

Boundaries and 12 Step Recovery

Old ways won't open new doors.

As a person who struggled with alcoholism and addiction for many years, I was very wary of 12 Step programs and the notion of "joining" anything. I had pretty much divorced myself from the human race for quite some time, had been in and out of countless treatment centers, and my consequences were piling up at an astounding rate. When it came to boundaries, mine had become quite warped and this was mostly due to alcohol and drug abuse, combined with a touch of narcissistic thinking. In the end I had lost nearly everything, which led to the first crack in my wall and eventually an entirely new perspective on life.

The first boundary that I made in recovery was with respect to drugs and alcohol themselves. It sounds obvious but it's worth stating. By boundary what we actually mean is abstinence. The 12-Step Program doesn't set out to teach you how to live normally with alcohol, it teaches you how to live normally without it. This is the hard reality that we have to accept: we have tried to moderate our drinking and we have failed. We thought that having 'control' over when and how much we drank was what we wanted until we saw that we were no longer controlling alcohol—it was controlling us. It is time to give up the fight and accept that the only way to regain control of our lives is to get rid of alcohol entirely - to put a firm and unmovable fence between ourselves and drink. Boundary #1.

I had had numerous experiences with people trying to force me to take Step 1 for several years. It doesn't work that way. This is the first step in recovery and it has to be taken by choice. When I accepted this great fact of self-responsibility, I became willing to take a look at some of my old ideas that perhaps hadn't been serving me well up to that point. For those who may have lived their lives in rebellion or in reaction to the imposition of others, working Step 1 may be one of the first self-directed experiences in memory. This "surrender" is the beginning of opening ourselves up to healthy change and learning how to relate to others and set limits is a big part of this.

Carla:

In early recovery, it became clear (as clear as anything could be in early recovery) that many of my perceptions were twisted by addictive thinking. I took some pretty drastic steps that may or may not be the right thing for others. First, I went in-patient, removing myself physically from those people and things that surrounded me in active addiction. Not everyone needs to do this, but I found it beneficial in facing only myself rather than myself in relation to others.

Second, when I left rehab, I didn't return to the relationship I had been in prior to treatment. At the time, I couldn't, really, though soon after, the opportunity to return was presented to me. I chose not to. His using was only one factor (albeit a large one). His insistence on controlling where I went and attempting to control what I thought was too much, and I knew I couldn't seek recovery on his terms. Third, I cut ties with people that I used with. They were mostly dealers and those I'd helped supply, though a few folks, finding I'd went to treatment, believed they were safe to come around me now that I had learned to "party responsibly" (I can chuckle now at the distorted perception that some normies have of our problem). I made it clear that I could not "party responsibly" and that under no circumstance could they bring it (whatever it might be) around me. My home is still a no-alcohol zone, though today, I don't automatically reject a social invitation if alcohol is served.

Those were all steps designed just to give me a chance at recovery without having temptation in my face. Other boundaries, I had to learn by talking to others who've had some practice living spiritual principles and who could help me to uncover my own motives. Like others say, the fourth step helps to uncover those motives, so until I get there, I learned to trust and rely on those who were farther along on the path.

Letting go of any semblance of control is a huge thing for nearly anyone, but most of all for alcoholics. Believe me, I get it. However, what I finally came to understand was that I was simply living under the delusion of control as I selfishly tried to control my circumstances and the actions of others, none of which ever worked out to my satisfaction. What did this leave me? Frustration on my part and pissed off family members all around. I think that the Big Book says it best and this is one of my favorite passages:

Selfishness - self-centeredness! That, we think, is the root of our troubles. Driven by a hundred forms of fear, self-delusion, self-seeking, and self-pity, we step on the toes of our fellows and they retaliate. Sometimes they hurt us, seemingly without provocation, but we invariably find that at some time in the past we have made decisions based on self which later placed us in a position to be hurt.

So our troubles, we think, are basically of our own making. They arise out of ourselves, and the alcoholic is an extreme example of self-will run riot, though he usually doesn't think so. Above everything, we alcoholics must be rid of this selfishness. We must, or it kills us! - Alcoholics Anonymous, P. 62

Now, I'd be remiss and really stating this out of context if I didn't give you the next line. "God makes that possible". Regardless of anyone's background, religious ideas, or lack thereof, I found that the only thing that is needed for recovery is some sort of belief in a higher power, something outside of myself that is in charge. I know that I tried everything under my own power for a good long time to either stop or control my drinking and using. I just couldn't do it. Then, later on, I tried the same with my character defects. Similarly disastrous results. There is no requirement in AA that one believes in God or in any specific conception of a Higher Power. Yes, there are mentions of "God" in the literature and even some Christian-based prayers that are said in the meetings. These aren't designed to trick you into converting to anything. A lot of this is born from Tradition and the roots of the program (good luck trying to change any of that).

Regardless, if you are Jewish, Catholic, Baptist, Atheist, or anything under the sun, there is no belief or "non-belief" system that AA has not been able to accommodate over the years. Atheists can use the power of the group (**G**roup **O**f **D**runks) as their higher power, others use **G**ood **O**rderly **D**irection, and still others use the impersonal force of nature. The only guiding principle is that the "higher power" must be a power greater than yourself, which all of these would certainly be.

While the Group of Drunks does work for many, AA does ask that members be willing to keep the door open to the possibility of a higher power that is spiritual in nature. This also does not dictate that members conform their beliefs to any particular God or religion. In fact, I've read a few things attributed to Bill W that said something along the lines of how glad he was when religious leaders from varied traditions found the Twelve Steps to be compatible with their religion. The concepts are ancient, and they existed before Christ. It is also quite common for this "belief" to develop and evolve over time, particularly as a result and byproduct of working the 12 Steps.

Yes, belief in a Higher Power can make life easier. I know that it goes against our very nature as alcoholics to want to give up any sort of control. Here is a list of benefits to consider in doing so:

- People who are attempting to escape a life of addiction can feel overwhelmed by that task and may have found that they don't have the ability to defeat their problem alone. In the AA program they can rely on a power greater than themselves to give them the strength they need.

- When people believe in a higher power they will usually find it easier to forgive other people who have wronged them. (i.e. - letting go of resentments and setting limits)

- The individual will need to face many challenges in recovery. It can be a great source of comfort to believe in a higher power that is providing them with help.

- In AA, they encourage members to learn how to let go. This means adopting a completely new approach to life. When people develop the ability to let go with the help of a higher power it brings them peace of mind and contentment.

- Belief in a higher power can give people a sense of purpose in their life. This new approach to life can strengthen their recovery and reduce the risk of relapse. Those who follow a spiritual path claim that it brings a great deal of happiness to their life.

- All spiritual paths encourage the individual to develop as humans. This will usually mean that they become more loving and mentally healthy. Addicts tend to be self-absorbed, but belief in a higher power can help to combat this tendency.

Again, this wasn't an overwhelming issue for me when I "joined" AA and committed to getting sober. I knew that my being "in charge" provided disastrous results and it was actually a relief to give up control, finally, in both the area of my addictions and in other matters in my life. This is an evolutionary process for most and my belief system has grown, evolved and enriched so much over the years. All it took in the beginning, however, was an ounce of willingness and I certainly had that.

When working the 12 Steps with a sponsor (recommended), the first true picture that we get of some of our defects and their effects on our relationships usually comes when we undertake a 4th Step. The passage that was quoted earlier from the Big Book was a prelude to this and much of what is discussed in AA's 12&12 deals with our relationships with others and how our "instincts run wild" have made us and those around us quite unhappy. In fact, there is so much in the 4th step literature as it relates to our total disregard for boundaries that it should become clear that much needs to change.

How frequently we see a frightened human being determined to depend completely upon a stronger person for guidance and protection. This weak one, failing to meet life's responsibilities with his own resources, never grows up. 12&12, P. 43

We have also seen men and women who go power-mad, who devote themselves to attempting to rule their fellows. These people often throw to the winds every chance for legitimate security and a happy family life. Whenever a human being becomes a battleground for the instincts, there can be no peace. 12&12, P. 44

Either we insist upon dominating the people we know, or we depend upon them far too much. If we lean too heavily on people, they will sooner or later fail us, for they are human, too, and cannot possibly meet our incessant demands. In this way our insecurity grows and festers. When we habitually try to manipulate others to our own willful desires, they revolt, and resist us heavily. Then we develop hurt feelings, a sense of persecution, and a desire to retaliate. As we redouble our efforts at control, and continue to fail, our suffering becomes acute and constant. We have not once sought to be one in a family, to be a friend among friends, to be a worker among workers, to be a useful member of society. Always we tried to struggle to the top of the heap, or to hide underneath it. This self-centered behavior blocked a partnership relation with any one of those about us. Of true brotherhood we had small comprehension. 12&12, P. 53

While the 4th step is a crucial one in recovery and particularly as it relates to discovering those underlying behavioral patterns that many of us had no idea existed, there is still much work to be done with regards to relationships with others and setting limits. As stated earlier, this Program is predicated on building a relationship with a power greater than yourself and the steps are designed to enable a person to do just that. No one need "try" to get this done. If the steps are worked as suggested, it simply happens. And when it does, it is this relationship that can help you achieve ongoing miracles in your recovery. It's happened for me and I continue to see it taking place with others on a daily basis.

Many relationships are healed that most thought beyond repair through the 8th and 9th Step. I know that my boundaries with regards to people who had "wronged" me were rigid and pretty ridiculous. As in - "You're dead to me". The steps allowed me to see where I had been incredibly selfish, self-centered, and oftentimes super rude. I made amends to people that I had sworn I would never speak to again and enjoy relationships with those people to this day, with healthy boundaries on both sides.

Since defective relations with other human beings have nearly always been the immediate cause of our woes, including our alcoholism, no field of investigation could yield more satisfying and valuable rewards than this one. Calm, thoughtful reflection upon personal relations can deepen our insight. We can go far beyond those things which were superficially wrong with us, to see those flaws which were basic, flaws which sometimes were responsible for the whole pattern of our lives. 12&12, P. 80

To define the word "harm" in a practical way, we might call it the result of instincts in collision, which cause physical, mental, emotional, or spiritual damage to people. 12&12, P. 80

It wasn't until I was at least five years sober and still having what I would consider to be some emotional sobriety issues that I really came to understand and appreciate the depth of the 6th and 7th steps. I had read the two paragraphs in the Big Book that dealt with these steps when I first worked them with my sponsor and even read "Drop the Rock" way back then, but the whole concept was really over my head at the time. The notion that I would have still have some glaring defects and relationship problems after years of not drinking was a bit discouraging to me - until I found out how very NOT alone I was.

In fact, emotional sobriety really is the "next frontier", as Bill W predicted and this is where the lifetime of work and steady growth lies. When I have been in pain in recovery, I have known what to do and have always come out the other side with a deeper insight about myself, my relationships with others, and my place in this world. This has almost always necessitated me working the steps again with a sponsor and really taking a great deal of time on Steps 6 & 7. If you haven't read "Drop the Rock", lately or ever, I highly suggest it.

Since most of us are born with an abundance of natural desires, it isn't strange that we often let these far exceed their intended purpose. When they drive us blindly, or we willfully demand that they supply us with more satisfactions or pleasures than are possible or due us, that is the point at which we depart from the degree of perfection that God wishes for us here on earth. That is the measure of our character defects, or, if you wish, of our sins. 12&12, P. 65

Indeed, the attainment of greater humility is the foundation principle of each of A.A.'s Twelve Steps. For without some degree of humility, no alcoholic can stay sober at all. Nearly all A.A.'s have found, too, that unless they develop much more of this precious quality than may be required just for sobriety, they still haven't much chance of becoming truly happy. Without it, they cannot live to much useful purpose, or, in adversity, be able to summon the faith that can meet any emergency. 12&12, P. 70

The chief activator of our defects has been self-centered fear—primarily fear that we would lose something we already possessed or would fail to get something we demanded. Living upon a basis of unsatisfied demands, we were in a state of continual disturbance and frustration. Therefore, no peace was to be had unless we could find a means of reducing these demands. The difference between a demand and a simple request is plain to anyone. The Seventh Step is where we make the change in our attitude which permits us, with humility as our guide, to move out from ourselves toward others and toward God. 12&12, P. 76

Anyone who actively works a 12 Step program will likely come to a point where a lot of these ideas and actions actually become second nature. It may take awhile but it does happen. What used to be the sick, old ideas, get replaced by healthier thinking and more positive actions. Even when we do continue behave in ways that don't serve our best interests with regards to relationships and boundaries, it generally becomes evident pretty quickly and we don't have to be too hard on ourselves.

Our first objective will be the development of self-restraint. This carries a top priority rating. When we speak or act hastily or rashly, the ability to be fair-minded and tolerant evaporates on the spot. One unkind tirade or one willful snap judgment can ruin our relation with another person for a whole day, or maybe a whole year. Nothing pays off like restraint of tongue and pen. We must avoid quick-tempered criticism and furious, power-driven argument. The same goes for sulking or silent scorn. These are emotional booby traps baited with pride and vengefulness. Our first job is to sidestep the traps. When we are tempted by the bait, we should train ourselves to step back and think. For we can neither think nor act to good purpose until the habit of self-restraint has become automatic. 12&12, P. 91

We can try to stop making unreasonable demands upon those we love. We can show kindness where we had shown none. With those we dislike we can begin to practice justice and courtesy, perhaps going out of our way to understand and help them. Whenever we fail any of these people, we can promptly admit it—to ourselves always, and to them also, when the admission would be helpful. Courtesy, kindness, justice, and love are the keynotes by which we may come into harmony with practically anybody. 12&12, P. 93

The fellowship of alcoholics anonymous is different than the 12 Steps but still valuable beyond measure. The fellowship is the bond that we have with other members of AA and this is shared both inside and outside of meetings. Whether sharing about successes or struggles with emotional sobriety and setting limitations, I have found that there is almost always someone else in the room or nearby that can relate to what I am going through. In fact, since I started working on this particular project, I have heard "boundaries" discussed more than I ever have in the past.

I was at a meeting just recently where a gentleman with over 30 years sober shared about his "lack of boundaries" and he lightheartedly poked fun at himself for still needing to work on something like that after so many years. Someone else was feeling good about herself for finally having the courage to set some much-needed boundaries with a family member. If we show up and stay open, we continue to get what we need. I know I do and it has brought me the freedom that I had been chasing with drugs and alcohol for so long.

So how does a boundary bring freedom? Because when you embrace sobriety, you receive your mind back. You have the power to say no. Alcohol is no longer your steamroller. And this is a freedom unlike the so-called freedom we think we had when we could drink 'whenever we wanted.' But there was a problem with that kind of freedom. We didn't have the choice to not drink whenever we wanted. Alcohol was the boss. In sobriety we take our lives and our decision-making capacity out of alcohol's hands and we reclaim it as our own.

We become free to make plans and keep them, to give our word and stick to it. We stop living in the shadows of broken promises and failed attempts and futility. When we get honest with alcohol, we get honest with ourselves and the rest of our lives and we become free.

Most of the principles of recovery contain a paradox and this concept is no different. But where has conventional wisdom or common sense ever gotten us? We have to reject the advice and the methods and the approaches that are not working for us and not serving our goal. You have the right to be free just as you have the right to be sober.

Fellowship as Family

There's a difference between a victim and a volunteer.

In some instances, through working the steps or other self-examination, we may find that our family of origin isn't as "normal" and healthy as we had previously thought. In fact, this is very common in recovery as many who wind up in the throes of addiction came from dysfunctional homes (there are exceptions) and sometimes abuse is also an issue. In these cases, this may be a sign that it's best for the ultimate boundaries to be put in place. Sometimes emotional distance is all that is called for and others it is best to break ties as much as possible.

One of the most amazing things about recovery fellowship members who face issues like this is the amount of support and love that they receive from other members. As I stated earlier, it's a virtual guarantee that someone close by has been through something similar in the past, no matter unique you think you or your situation may be. This allows the person suffering to get a caring hand with relevant experience and to see that there is hope on the other side. Even those who don't have experience with similar issues generally rally around someone who is suffering and the relief felt by the one in pain is almost immediate.

While we may not always get the love and support that we need from our family of origin, that love and support is available to us from other people if we remain open to it. No one need be alone on a holiday who is a member of a 12 Step fellowship. There are countless opportunities to be of service to others and to get outside of yourself and your own problems, giving back what has been so freely given to you. When the proper boundaries are in place in your life, these are the gifts and the promises that will continue to materialize under all conditions.

Stephanie:

I have cut my ties with my toxic family almost ten years ago. I grew up with a lot of emotional abuse which led to physical towards the end. It was a tough decision for me to make but it was the best I ever could have done. Till this day, they don't see the extent of what they did wrong and I do not want any part of that. Distancing myself allowed me to heal emotionally, pursue my goals, and to live the life I deserve. I am currently married to an amazing man and one day soon we will have children of our own in a loving, supporting environment. It's true, you may forget what people say or do, but you don't forget how people make you feel regardless of who they are. It really is a difficult choice to make, but for me it had made me stronger, it made me grow as a person and in actuality it made me happier. Be around people who bring you up, not bring you down even if it is family.

Outside Help

The real risk is doing nothing.

Many people in recovery struggle in dealing what we call "outside issues". Some of these, such as other addictive behaviors, can be dealt with by working the Steps or through participation in another fellowship. Still others cannot and this is where confusion often sets in. The other issues that may be affecting a person's recovery and emotional sobriety may have been known in advance, may not come to light until well into sobriety, or may have been neglected for a time as a person stopped taking care of themselves or working their program. The fact is that alcoholics and addicts can be pretty complicated folks, and despite AAs success in helping alcoholics get and stay sober, AA alone is not enough to manage the host of complications that an alcoholic may have. That is why AA is very clear about separating itself from medicine and psychiatry, pointedly telling members to get "outside help" when necessary.

Research has proven that people with alcohol or other drug disorders often suffer from a bouquet of descriptive acronyms and psycho jargon that has replaced AAs placid "character defects" mentioned so often in the Big Book - "duel disorders," "comorbid disorders," "MICA" (mentally ill chemical abusers) and substance abusers with "SMI" (serious mental health illness), to name a few. The newest term is "co-occurring disorder." The percentages are a bit daunting as well; about 16% of the US population suffers from substance abuse problems. In people with mental health disorders, the number is almost twice as high: 29%. Forty-seven percent of schizophrenics and 56% of people with bipolar disorders have a substance abuse disorder. Almost 80% of alcoholics experience depression at some time in their lives, and 30% meet the diagnostic requirements for major depression. As many as one-third of people entering treatment for substance abuse issues meet the requirements for Post-Traumatic Stress Syndrome (PTSD).

So how does a member know when it is time to seek "outside help"? Well, if you have been handed one of those nifty diagnoses either before getting sober, in treatment, or sometime since that would be a good indication that you may want to check in with your doctor and let them know what's up. If you don't have a specialist, just start with a General Practitioner and be honest about your situation and where you are at. A great mental health professional for recovering addicts are LADC's (Licensed Alcohol and Drug Counselor), which many times can either be psychiatrists or medical doctors with additional training in chemical dependency and abuse issues. It's well-known that diagnosing and treating many "co-concurring" disorders can be difficult until the patient has been sober at least 6 months, when you can get a clearer picture of what they are really like.

While managing boundaries can become very difficult under these circumstances, one of the many dangers of not managing co-occurring disorders, of course, is relapse. Active addiction amplifies the co-occurring disorders so that sobriety must indeed come first if the sufferer is going to have any hope of getting better. But the other side is that untreated depression, anxiety or mania can trigger relapse. The American Association of Marriage and Family Therapists has set up an online service for people in recovery to "seek outside help." The TherapistLocator.net website is designed specifically to put those in need of services in touch with those who provide them. If you feel like you need Outside Help, don't be afraid to get it.

Living a Healthy Life with Boundaries

*Your personal boundaries protect the inner
core of your identity and your right to choices.
– Gerard Manley Hopkins*

Setting clear personal boundaries is the key to ensuring relationships are mutually respectful, supportive and caring. Boundaries are a measure of self-esteem. They set the limits for acceptable behavior from those around you, determining whether they feel able to put you down, make fun, or take advantage of your good nature.

If you often are made uncomfortable by others' treatment of you, it may be time to reset these boundaries to a more secure level. Weak boundaries leave you vulnerable and likely to be taken for granted or even damaged by others. On the other hand, a healthy self-respect will produce boundaries which show you deserve to be treated well. They also will protect you from exploitative relationships and help you avoid getting too close to people who don't have your recovery and best interests at heart.

Healthy Boundaries

Appropriate boundaries create integrity. –
Rae Shagalov

Even if you've done a lot of spiritual work, you may still allow others to violate your boundaries or you may violate those of others. You may know people who chronically disrupt boundaries but have never realized it or deny it. You may even be enabling their behavior. Fortunately, you can dramatically improve in this area through conscious practice, honesty, and patience.

Beware, though, of underestimating the challenge of setting and maintaining healthy limits. Boundary issues are more complex than just inappropriate language or action, and their complexities are revealed only after you have some clarity. Mastering the issue of boundaries does not happen all at once; it's a gradual process that eventually leads to a more authentic and powerful you. Here are the qualities that relationships (not just romantic ones) with healthy boundaries exhibit.

First, they are relationships in which each person can say no without fear of punishment. If you are able to set limits without worry about losing the relationship or being treated poorly, the relationship has good boundaries. On the other hand, if you worry about saying no, it may be time to look at what you fear about saying no. Do you fear loss of the relationship, the silent treatment, or an angry reaction? Positive relationships are those in which you can say both yes and no freely.

Second, one person does not rely solely on the other for all emotional needs. If a "no" from a friend means that you are devastated, it may be time to look more deeply at how you get your needs met. It is too much to expect that one single person can meet all of your needs for safety, security and love. Having internal strength and support from a variety of sources will allow you to set and accept boundaries more easily.

Third, each person takes responsibility for meeting their own needs, but are responsible to each other. As human beings, we have a responsibility to help each other when burdens become too heavy. When a family member, friend or co-worker is overwhelmed or going through difficult times, we are responsible to care for each other. However, when we take over someone else's responsibility and do not allow them to do what they are capable of, we cross boundaries. Often times, when this occurs, we need to look at our motives, as we may do this more for our own gain than for the other person.

Fourth, each can ask for and accept help from the other without keeping score. Neither feels resentful about their part in the relationship. In strong relationships, there is give and take so each person feels cared about. They are able to share weaknesses so each feels loved for who they are without having to pretend they can do it all alone.

Finally, people in relationships with healthy boundaries say yes when they mean yes and no when they mean no. Being able to say and hear "no" is freeing because it means you are free to say and hear "yes" as well. You can be secure in the knowledge that when the other person says "yes," they mean it. You trust that they are not burdened because if they were, they would say no!

As you explore your most important relationships, do they meet these qualifications whether they are family, friends or work relationships? Do you feel taken advantage of or is there give and take? If you find yourself in a relationship with unhealthy boundaries, it may be time to take a closer look at the limits you are setting – or not setting. Remember, you can only change you, not the other person. Whether at home, with friends or in the workplace, healthy boundaries are the key to relationships that enrich your life rather than drain you of energy.

The first step in learning to set boundaries is self-awareness and, as people in recovery, we get better and better at this as time goes on. For example, pay close attention to the situations when you lose energy, feel a knot in your stomach, or want to cry. Identifying where you need more space, self-respect, energy or personal power is the first step. If you are still having trouble identifying your boundaries, try completing these three sentences with at least 10 examples (note the examples given).

1. **People many not...**

- Go though my personal belongings
- Criticize me
- Make comments about my weight
- Take their anger out on me
- Humiliate me in front of others
- Tell off-color jokes in my company
- Invade my personal space

2. **I have a right to ask for...**

- Privacy
- A new hairstyle from an old stylist
- Peace and quiet while getting a massage
- Help around the house
- More information before making a purchase
- Quiet time to myself

3. To protect my time and energy, it's OK to...

- Turn the ringer off on the phone
- Take my time returning calls or e-mails
- Change my mind
- Bow out of a volunteer activity
- Cancel a commitment when I'm not feeling well
- Reserve a place in my home that is off-limits to others.

Remember the importance of saying "no" to unreasonable requests, and reasonable ones from time to time, if they conflict with your plans. Challenge all insults that are masked as humor. As you learn to extend your boundaries, try to adapt your behavior so you are not stepping over other people's. This may take an extra effort because our habits can go unnoticed, but aim to stop making digs at people, or using humor as a weapon to put others down.

The 'Five Things' Method

- List five things you'd like people to stop doing around you, for example, gossiping about people who aren't present

- List five things you want people to stop doing to you, for example, being rude or inconsiderate, or ignoring you

Boundaries in Recovery

- List five things that people may no longer say to you, for example, "you always give up" or "you'll never get promoted"

Think about your current boundaries and ask:

- how much attention people expect from you at a moment's notice

- whether you always make yourself available (e.g. do you answer the phone no matter what's going on?)

- how much praise and acceptance you receive

- why you are popular with your friends

- how you feel after spending time with each friend or family member

Consider how these things make you feel as you answer these questions and as you go onto the last section of the book. Remember that boundaries work both ways: they create emotional health and are created by people with emotional health. They are something you can start working on today with the people close to you and you'll begin to notice a difference in your self-esteem, confidence, emotional stability, and so on.

Personal Bill of Rights

*Let Life race you out beyond your own
boundaries over and over again until you are
comfortable with watching the map of
normal's edge disappear behind you.
Let Life show you that it is safe to exceed your
own expectations and reputation and prove
that the only danger in following her into the
wilderness is a loss of your own fear.
This is when we gain the warrior's heart, the
master's eye, and the student's mind. After
that, Life holds our hand in every adventure
and shows us things not possible before. – Jacob
Nordby*

By a certain stage in our recovery we begin to discover that we have rights as individual human beings. As children and even as adults we may have been treated by others as though we had few or no rights. We, ourselves, may have come to believe that we had no rights, had rights that we really didn't, and we may be living our lives now as though we have some false ideas about personal rights. As we recover, however, we can put together our own personal "Bill of Rights" that can confirm for us the rights that we do in fact have. We give up those rights only if we decide to and this has everything to with boundaries and emotional sobriety. You may wish to consider whether you have any of these rights, and any others that come to mind. Many of us put this list of rights in a conspicuous place where we can read it often.

I HAVE THE RIGHT TO:

• To ask for what I want.

• To refuse requests or demands I can't meet.

• To express all of my feelings, positive or negative.

• To change my mind.

• To make mistakes and not have to be perfect.

• To follow my own values and standards.

• To say no to anything when I feel I am not ready, it is unsafe, or it violates my values.

• To have no contact with someone who hurts me physically or emotionally and I have a

right to take whatever steps are necessary to achieve this.

• To determine my own priorities.

• To not be responsible for others' behavior, actions, feelings, or problems.

• To expect honesty from others.

• To be angry at someone I love.

• To be uniquely myself.

• To feel scared and say "I'm afraid."

• To say "I don't know."

• To not give excuses or reasons for my behavior.

• To make decisions based on my feelings.

• To my own needs for personal space and time.

• To time alone even if others want me to spend it with them

• To be playful and frivolous.

• To be healthier than those around me.

• To be in a non-abusive environment.

• To be trusted and not have my integrity questioned. If my trust was deliberately violated by anyone I have a right to choose to walk away and have my choice respected. Or I can choose to carefully access my risks and allow the person to try to rebuild my trust. In that case I have a right to let the person know the boundaries required to do this.

• To hold others accountable for their own behavior and not let them shift the blame to
me.

• To NOT let others use guilt or pity or shame to manipulate me. I am only responsible
for my OWN behavior.

• To NOT feel guilty for not behaving as others might want me to or for not giving
others what they expect from me.

• To make friends and be comfortable around people.

• To change and grow.

• To forgive others and to forgive myself.

• To decide what I want to share with others about matters that concern me and that is
determined by what feels right to me--not what they want.

• To grieve over actual or threatened losses

• To be flexible and comfortable with doing so

• To grieve over what I didn't get that I needed or what I got that I didn't need or want –
and to let it go once I have

• To have my needs and wants respected by others.

• To be treated with dignity and respect.

• To be Happy! :)

Look through the list and, at first, circle the statements that grab your attention. From that list, pick a couple that you would like to incorporate into your life. You can even start with just one statement, play with it, get used to the idea of it, try it out, and then add others as your confidence grows! Rewrite the statement if needed and make it yours.

Read the statement out loud, and reflect: "Do I really believe this now?" If the answer is "No" or "I'm not sure," ask yourself "Why not?" What doesn't feel right about the statement? What would happen if you owned that belief – include the positive and the negative? The thoughts and feelings coming up will make great targets for reflection and future work. Acknowledge that, while you may not have been taught some of these beliefs as a child, you can adopt them today. Affirming your personal rights repeatedly will help free you of old inhibitions and distorted beliefs, and empower you to learn how to be firmly assertive (vs. aggressive or submissive) with others in a clear, positive, and respectful way.

Remember, you'll set boundaries when you are ready and not a minute sooner. There is a satisfying side to setting boundaries... you'll find that you're attracting people into your life who value you as you value yourself.

Afterward

Expose yourself to your deepest fear; after that, fear has no power, and the fear of freedom shrinks and vanishes. You are free. — *Jim Morrison*

Breaking free from addiction is a difficult thing, both for the addict and those close to them. I was a person who had to have something to change the way they felt for many years, not understanding that the drugs and the alcohol weren't the solution I believed them to be. When I finally surrendered and got sober, I started to learn some hard truths about myself. I had been living in fear for so long that I no longer knew how to have a healthy relationship with another human being, if I ever had this ability in the first place.

It took many years and much trial and error to come to the conclusion that emotional sobriety and setting limitations needed to be a key focus on my journey going forward. As addiction at its core is a failure to regulate emotions, recovery needs to include the growing up process of learning how to function as a mature adult with proper boundaries. As a sober, dignified, person you get to find your courage, decide how you want to live, protect yourself and your recovery, and live an authentic life. Boundaries can help you do all of these things. My best to you. - Taite A.

Resources

Treatment Centers

There are no "public" websites that offer treatment center, detox and sober living directories. Unfortunately, any site you find will be filled with "sponsored results". This means rehabs that have paid for ad space. That's not always a bad thing, just not an unbiased thing. If you still need help with this, the best site I've found is Sober.com. You'll get the sponsored results in your search but you will also get all of the public listings as well, including the government-funded (some free) facilities.

Support Groups

<u>Primary:</u>
Alcoholics Anonymous (http://aa.org/)
Narcotics Anonymous (http://www.na.org/)
Cocaine Anonymous (http://ca.org/)
Co-Dependence Anonymous (CoDA) (http://www.coda.org/)
Gamblers Anonymous (http://www.gamblersanonymous.org/ga/)
Sex and Love Addicts Anonymous (http://www.slaafws.org/)
Overeaters Anonymous (http://www.oa.org/)
Eating Disorders Anonymous (http://www.eatingdisordersanonymous.org/index.htm)

<u>For Families:</u>
Al-Anon Websites (http://www.al-anon.alateen.org/)
Nar-Anon Family Groups (http://www.nar-anon.org/naranon/)
Families Anonymous (http://www.familiesanonymous.org/)
Children of Addicts (http://mdjunction.com/children-of-addicts)
Gam-Anon (http://www.gam-anon.org/)

Mental Health

National Institute of Mental Health (http://www.nimh.nih.gov/)
Results of biomedical research on mind and behavior.

National Alliance for the Mentally Ill (http://www.nami.org/)
Support for consumers with mental illness

Substance Abuse & Mental Health Services Administration
(http://www.samhsa.gov/)
United States Department of Health & Human Services

Government Resources

Single-State Agency (SSA) Directory:
(http://www.recoverymonth.gov/Recovery-Month-
Kit/Resources/Single-State-Agency-SSA-Directory.aspx)
Prevention and Treatment of Substance Use and Mental Disorders – A
list of State offices that can provide local information and guidance
about substance use and mental disorders, treatment, and recovery in
your community.

AMVETS (http://www.amvets.org/)
This organization provides support for veterans and the active military
in procuring their earned entitlements. It also offers community
services that enhance the quality of life for this Nation's citizens.

Professionals

Intervention Project for Nurses (http://www.ipnfl.org/)
Help for professionals with chemical dependencies.

International Lawyers in Alcoholics Anonymous (ILAA)
(http://www.ilaa.org/)
This organization serves as a clearinghouse for support groups for lawyers who are recovering from alcohol or other chemical dependencies.

International Pharmacists Anonymous (IPA)
(http://home.comcast.net/~mitchfields/ipa/ipapage.htm)
This is a 12-step fellowship of pharmacists and pharmacy students recovering from any addiction.

Gambling

National Council on Problem Gambling
(http://www.ncpgambling.org/)
Disseminates information about problem and pathological (compulsive) gambling. Also, promotes the development of services for those with the disorder.

GamCare - (http://www.gamecare.org.uk)
The UK's national organisation for gambling. Offers a telephone help line for people with gambling problems in the United Kingdom. Also, offers an Internet chat help line.

Other

This Center for Substance Abuse Prevention widget (http://www.samhsa.gov/about/csap.aspx) includes a variety of updates on activities relating to underage drinking which is updated regularly with local, state, and national articles published by online sources.

NCADD: (http://ncadd.org/)
The National Council on Alcoholism and Drug Dependence, Inc. (NCADD) and its Affiliate Network is a voluntary health organization dedicated to fighting the Nation's #1 health problem – alcoholism, drug addiction and the devastating consequences of alcohol and other drugs on individuals, families and communities.

American Council for Drug Education (http://www.acde.org/)
Educational programs and services for teens, parents, and educators

Faces & Voices of Recovery: (http://www.facesandvoicesofrecovery.org/)
Faces & Voices of Recovery is dedicated to organizing and mobilizing the over 23 million Americans in recovery from addiction to alcohol and other drugs, our families, friends and allies into recovery community organizations and networks, to promote the right and resources to recover through advocacy, education and demonstrating the power and proof of long-term recovery.

About the Author

Taite Adams grew up everywhere. The only child of an Air Force navigator and school teacher, moving around became second nature by grade school. By age 20, she was an alcoholic, drug addict and self-proclaimed egomaniac. Pain is a great motivator, as is jail, and she eventually got sober has found peace and joy in this life beyond measure.

At the age of 42, Taite published her first book titled "Kickstart Your Recovery". Now permanently Free on Amazon, the book answers many of the questions that she herself had but was afraid to ask before giving up the fight with addiction and entering recovery over a decade prior. Since, she has published four other recovery books, including her bestselling book on Opiate Addiction, and has moved into the broader spirituality and self-help genres.

Leading a spiritual life is all about choices. The practice of spiritual principles and the willingness to remain teachable are the key ingredients for growth. As a spiritual seeker and reader of the self-help genre herself, Taite appreciates and respects each and every person who takes the time to read her works and respond with reviews and comments. For more information on books, upcoming releases, and to connect with the author, go to http://www.taiteadams.com.

Check out our active Facebook Page: Taite Adams.

Boundaries in Recovery

As you begin your Road to Recovery, please check out Taite's first book, Kickstart Your Recovery, available in both Kindle (where's it is Permanently FREE) and Paperback.

Should you require additional assistance with your home detox, be sure to pick up Taite's popular book, Safely Detox From Alcohol and Drugs at Home, also on Amazon.com.

Opiate Addiction has reached epidemic proportions in this country and is something that Taite is intimately familiar with. Read her bestselling book on this topic, chronicling this insidious killer and laying the pathway for freedom from its grip.

Benzodiazepine Addiction is fast becoming a problem of epidemic proportions world-wide, and it's one that crosses all age barriers. Beyond Benzos examines this serious prescription drug addiction and its complicated detox options.

Senior Addiction refers to the growing issue of alcoholism and drug addiction amongst older adults. As baby boomers hit retirement age in record numbers, the instances of overdose deaths and new treatment admissions in this age group is skyrocketing. Read about the particular issues with regards to addiction and treatment in this particular class.

If you or a loved one are in recovery from alcoholism or addiction and want to learn more about emotional sobriety, check out Taite's book titled Restart Your Recovery, also on Amazon.com.

It's hard to miss mention in the media of the drug Molly and the controversy surrounding it's use and it's ingredients. There is plenty of confusion there as well. Check out Taite's latest book, called Who is Molly? for the latest info on this drug and it's dangers.

Have you ever wanted to learn more about Ego? Taite's latest book, titled <u>E-Go: Ego Distancing Through Mindfulness, Emotional Intelligence & The Language of Love</u>, takes an in depth look at ego. Consider how you define yourself and how to live a happier life, apart from ego in your career, relationships, and health.

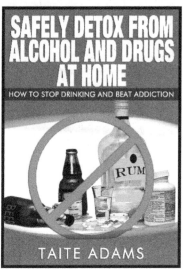

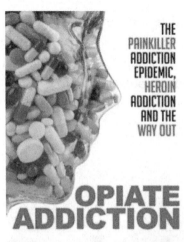

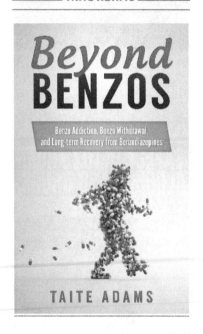

Made in United States
Orlando, FL
03 June 2024